# Jesus of Nazareth

# JESUS
# OF NAZARETH

*Meditations on His Humanity*

JOSE COMBLIN

*Translated by Carl Kabat, O.M.I.*

ORBIS BOOKS
MARYKNOLL    NEW YORK

Second Paperback Printing, December 1982
ISBN 0-88344-239-6

Originally published as *Jesus de Nazaré* by Editora Vozes
Ltda., R. Frei Luis, 100, 25.600 Petrópolis, R.J., Brazil

Copyright © 1976 Orbis Books, Maryknoll, New York
10545

Library of Congress Catalog Card Number: 75-29580
ISBN: 0-88344-231-0

Manufactured in the United States of America

# CONTENTS

# *Introduction*

The reader has the right to ask some words of explanation. In this book we intend to meditate on the human—simply human—life of Jesus Christ. We want to examine again this Jesus of Nazareth just as the disciples knew him and understood him—or did not understand him—when they walked with him in the rough valleys of Galilee, roaming the villages of Israel, when they did not yet know him as Lord and Son of God. We want to see this Jesus just as he appeared when he had not yet manifested his personal bond with God: when, to the eyes of the disciples, he was still only a man.

We are aware of the objections of the theologians and of all the specialists. They can be reduced to three fundamental problems: the biographical impasse, the theological ferment of the primitive Christian community, and the modern conception of the act of faith.

First, the biographical impasse. Some fifty

1

years ago, the school called "Form Criticism" proved in a definitive way the impossibility of writing a biography of Jesus. The critics showed that the gospels were composed of collections of small units that occurred independently one from another. It was established that the sequence of the units in the redaction of the gospels had nothing to do with the historical succession of events, and therefore, the critics maintained, there is no certain way to reestablish the order of the events in Jesus' life. Each evangelist—and even before the evangelists, the authors of the collections they used—reunited the units in the terms of content. This proposition may be considered as definitive, and the Second Vatican Council accepted it without difficulty. Consequently, a biography of Jesus in the sense we usually understand the word  is impossible to unite. Nevertheless, this does not obviate the possibility of reconstructing the outlines of the personality of Jesus or a general impression of his way of acting. Even if we ignore the question of the order of events, these facts exist  and permit us to derive an idea of his human personality, particularly if we take into account the fact that all the events were lived within a very short period of some three years at the most.

Second objection: We are aware that all the recollections, all the oral traditions about the life of Jesus were reviewed, re-thought, elaborated upon by the first Christians. This work continued for almost fifty years until the definitive edition of our gospels. The first Christians and their successors related the facts and the sayings of Jesus with the significance and perception that they themselves, illuminated by the Spirit, had of the transmitted material. The differences among the gospels show with what liberty the Christians repeated the facts they received. It is therefore possible to infer that the evangelical units reflect not only the understanding of the primitive tradition, but also the theological comprehension of the Christian communities.

Up to a certain point, the faith of the disciples, the explanations or the insinuations made by them in the content of the oral tradition constitute a curtain that separates us from the pure historical reality. It is true that the cases are very few in which we are able with some certainty to believe we hear the "proper words" of Jesus (the exact words). Few, too, are the cases in which we can have absolute confidence in the details of the narrations. Many words, many particulars are based on the reflection of faith of the first Christians, rather than the journalistic report of the bare facts. Here also Vatican II has accepted the conclusions of the specialists.

Nevertheless, even with all this filtration and all these elaborations of the details and the words, the person of Jesus, his human personality and presence shine forth with such a force that a true picture of him is unmistakable. If, for example, one considers the phrases of the Sermon on the Mount separately—though every one is doubtful individually—the total impression is so original that no variation of details can invalidate it. This impression is not the result of an elaboration by the primitive community; rather it springs from an experience that even the most fertile imagination could not possibly have invented. The best proof of the historicity of the figure of Jesus which comes down to us is the impossibility of inventing such a figure. Where could anyone find a poet, a novelist, capable of such invention?

Third objection: We are aware that faced with the impossibility of constructing a biography, many contemporary theologians have decided to place little emphasis on the life of the historical Jesus. This is so even though Saint

Paul clearly distinguishes between the Christ of the flesh and the Christ according to the Spirit. But if all Christians were to accept this concept of Jesus, the Christian faith would have for its exclusive object the resurrected Christ, without reference to historical facts; and the Jesus of the gospels would be confined to the glorified Christ. Faith would be an option for God—the God manifested in the resurrected Christ. It would be simply to proclaim that "Christ is Lord."

Of course, we do not doubt that the ultimate expression of the Christian faith is the recognition that God raised Jesus from the dead and thus manifested to us his divine sonship. However, the experience of centuries teaches us the danger inherent in a faith which seeks to arrive immediately at its term, without passing through the preparatory stages. To arrive at the point of confessing the resurrection of Christ, and of proclaiming with Saint John that he is the Son of God, does not mean that we can skip over this prior phase. True it may be that the apostles finally reached faith in Christ resurrected. But before this they knew Jesus for three years in the flesh, and during those three years God left them in ignorance of Jesus' essential nature. First they experienced the companionship of Jesus, the man. Today we also find it useful first to travel the steps of companionship with the human—simply human—life of Jesus, before arriving at a definitive act of faith.

We now know too well how easy it is to obscure our act of faith by substituting the formation of a myth of Christ for real faith in him. We know how easy it is also to make of faith an act of blind option, a leap into the pure mystery of God, a pure desire without intellectual content, without representation. But real Christian faith matures little by little, after a long journey with Jesus, starting from the evangelical recollections. After all, the message of Saint Paul did not lead the first Christians to think that the gospels would be dispensable in the future. Although in a certain way it may be easier for some people to throw themselves into an act of adherence to the God revealed in Christ than it is to accompany the simply human life of Jesus and assimilate its content, the spirituality of centuries shows the danger of illusion which accompanies a metaphysical leap to Christ's divinity that is made without dedicating sufficient time to meditation on his humanity.

The humanity of Jesus Christ must never be considered as a garb which God put on to make himself visible. It is a truly human life, whose human significance constitutes the key to knowing the true God. This Son of God, in whom we affirm that we believe, would be either myth or illusion if we did not first of all exhaust the substance of the facts and of the sayings of Jesus, collected for us in the gospels.

We are well aware of the technical difficulties implicit in the interpretation of the gospels, and, in a particular way, of the words and the acts of Jesus. Therefore, we shall, insofar as possible, avoid the controversial subjects and the affirmations subject to serious conflicts. Instead, we shall attempt to limit our consideration to the facts which we feel can be affirmed with serious probability. Nor do we consider it proper here to present the technical arguments which sustain our positions. Readers can easily find them in specialized works.

It is, however, necessary to examine with special care the Gospel according to John. No one doubts the historicity of the abundant information given by John. On the other hand, no one defends the word-by-word historicity of the "discourses." These "discourses " of a style so different from the words of the Synoptic Gospels are apparently much later compositions—probably from around the end of the first century. They certainly contain authentic quotations; but no one could possibly attribute every single word of any one of them to Jesus. In a general way, therefore, we will leave the grand discourses of the fourth Gospel to one side. They have more value as meditations on the Christology taught by John than as a meditation on the simply human life of Jesus.

In the present book of meditations, therefore, we will follow the texts of the gospels as exactly as possible—especially that of Mark, the oldest of them all. We will avoid projecting personal sentiments, devotional expressions, or pious interpretations without historic foundation into these texts. The literary style of meditation used to be the privileged place for gratuitous exegeses. It was useful for arousing sentiments of praiseworthy piety, and certain persons were able to find consolation, discovering in the gospels the sentiments that they projected. But such an exercise is totally foreign to the sense of the gospel texts, as we will attempt to consider them here.

# CHAPTER 1

# *The Man*

## JESUS' FAMILY

There is no obscurity about the ancestry of Jesus: He was from Nazareth of Galilee, son of a modest family, with nothing unusual about his background, apparently much like any son of a humble artisan in a small town. The absence of mystery in Jesus' origin was later called to the attention of the people who listened to him: "Yet we all know where he comes from" (John 7:27). If he was a descendant of David, in accord with the genealogies the evangelists added at a much later date to the narrative of his acts, or if at the time he was born there were extraordinary happenings, these facts were unknown to his followers. To the eyes of those to whom he began preaching there was nothing especially extraordinary about him. He was only the son of a poor family.

For about thirty years, Jesus immersed himself in the life of a humble family of the insignificant town of Nazareth, apparently so like his relatives and seeming so ordinary to his co-citizens that it totally amazed those who knew him when he suddenly separated himself from them and began his ministry. His neighbors said at the time, "This is the carpenter's son, surely. Is he not the son of the woman called Mary, and the brother of James and Joseph and Simon and Jude? His sisters, too, are they not all here with us?" (Matthew 13:55–56). "They would not accept him" (Mark 6:4). Their incomprehension was so complete that one day they expelled him from the synagogue of Nazareth (Luke 4:28). Seeing the agitation and enthusiasm Jesus provoked among the Jews who had not grown up with him, his relatives were shamed or fearful before their neighbors. When he returned home, he was followed by so great a multitude that they were not even able to eat. And his family, when they heard of this, "set out to take charge of him, convinced he was out of his mind" (Mark 3:20–21).

Much later, however, when they saw his success lasted, his relatives began to perceive the advantages that might accrue to them from the fame of a cousin who brought distinction to his house. They said to him: "Why not leave this place and go to Judaea, and let your disciples see the works you are doing; if a man wants to be known he does not do things in secret; since you are doing all this, you should let the whole world see" (John 7:3–4). They spoke as relatives of a young politician speak when they see he has succeeded sufficiently in his small town that he could launch himself in the capital—as if, for instance, he had wanted to run for senator.

In his turn, Jesus did not feel at all held back by his family. From the moment he began his mission, his family, as such, seemed to cease to exist for him. He showed neither resentment nor attachment to it; he sought no family privileges, did not intrude in family business. He did not even choose to be its religious counselor. Once his mission projected him onto the world scene, he gave himself to all people, and all people were his family: "His mother and brothers now arrived and, standing outside, sent in a message asking for him. A crowd was sitting round him at the time the message was passed to him, 'Your mother and brothers and sisters are outside asking for you.' Jesus replied, 'Who are my mother and my brothers?' And looking at those seated in a circle around him he said, 'Here are my mother and my brothers. Anyone who does the will of God, that person is my brother and sister and mother' " (Mark 3:32–35).

## HIS FORMATION

Jesus was a carpenter. He had received the usual formation that the artisans of Galilee received. When he started on his ministry, therefore, those who had known him previously were amazed. They asked themselves, "Where did he get all this? What kind of wisdom is he endowed with? How is it that such miraculous deeds are accomplished by his hands?" (Mark 6:2). In his own city, "all who were present spoke favorably of him; they marveled at the appealing discourse which came from his lips. They also asked, 'Is not this Joseph's son?' " (Luke 4:22).

He came from Galilee, the province farthest from the capital and most backward culturally.

From the point of view of the Judaic religion, Galilee was also a region where the religious law was applied with less rigor. Nothing in its tradition predestined it to carry out any role in the destiny of the nation. As Nathaniel said: "Can anything good come from Nazareth?" (John 1:46). The other Jews said in their turn: "Surely the Messiah is not to come from Galilee?" (John 7:41). And they said to Nicodemus: "Look it up. You will not find the prophet coming from Galilee" (John 7:52). Even the Galileans' provincial accent, like a rural accent today, was a cause for ridicule of them among the Jews (Matthew 26:73).

Jesus had studied the Bible in the local synagogue with all the little boys of his town. But he did not frequent the rabbinical schools in which the youth of the good families, such as Paul, had been able to prepare themselves for the career of scribe or other dominant roles in their society. He was not prepared to exercise any office among his people or in his religion. He never had contact with the priestly families. In the temple, he appeared to be only another lay pilgrim from the countryside, a pilgrim of Galilee who came to fulfill his vows. Naturally the city-bred Jews were scandalized when this "unsophisticated" pilgrim spoke and disturbed the order of the temple without having received any permission to speak from the authorities.

Jesus presumably had learned to read and write a little just as the other young boys of his circumstances did—enough at least, to be able to read the scriptures. Most of his culture, however, was of an oral type. Any skill he may have had in writing he did not use to communicate with his people. He never wrote his message.

On the other hand, we should not dismiss out of hand the value and the depth of the biblical culture he had received. He was not stupid. Furthermore, study of the scriptures gave the Jews a vision of the world and of history, a wisdom and a rich vocabulary, precious instruments to express the sense of the life and the destiny of a people. Jesus did not need any infusion of new concepts. The culture received in the synagogue was sufficient to encourage him to propagate his message. Because he was a Jew, Jesus knew his traditions, and he knew that he knew them. They compared more than adequately with those of the pagans and the Samaritans. He himself said as much to the Samaritan woman: "You worship what you do not know; we worship what we do know; for salvation comes from the Jews" (John 4:22).

He was aware that he belonged to a superior people, a unique people although one humiliated for centuries by foreigners. The Judaic culture, in fact, gave him advantages he would not have received in a pagan land. He was not a slave, nor did he have slaves. In Nazareth all were free, and all were conscious of being brothers and sisters in the same alliance in which Moses united the tribes of Israel. It was, of course, possible to have injustices in Nazareth. The people, however, knew they were injustices and did not call good evil, nor evil good. They all believed in the promises of justice and peace made by the prophets. It is, in fact, impossible to overestimate Jesus' Judaic formation. It was the basic formation we ought to give our own children: the entire Old Testament, in its mentality, its hopes, in its incessant ferment of denunciation, protest, anxieties, aspirations, witness, and prophecy.

Jesus completely assimilated this biblical culture. He identified himself with the sentiments of the Old Testament and meditated on it so profoundly that all his thought was nothing else than an expression of scripture—with the single difference that he did not feel himself constrained by the letter of the law. Instead, he dominated the law to such a point that he was able to cite it freely, without fear of error about its deepest sense. And more remarkably he knew how to distinguish between the real substance of the word of God and the concessions which Moses had given to the Jews because they "were so unteachable" (Mark 10:5).

Jesus was perfectly aware of the extraordinary liberty the biblical message confers on people before the powers of the world. Not even the immense power of Caesar impressed him. Pagans trembled; Romans accepted domination; the people of their empire accepted slavery. But the Jews did not accept it. Even a simple Jewish carpenter like himself could not be intimidated by the "glory that was Rome." In this, of course, Jesus was not unique. It is enough to read the books of the Maccabees or the list of revolts of the Jews against the successive occupiers of the land of their ancestors to be sure of that.

As a Jew, Jesus had learned also that all the children of Israel were brothers and sisters and were equal. Among them, it was not possible to

have oppressors and oppressed. As a matter of
fact, it is from this consciousness of familyhood, unique in its time, that today all our
consciousness of social solidarity derives.

## HIS VOCATION

How then was the idea of Jesus' vocation
born and how did it develop in his mind? We do
not really know. It is a notable fact that rarely in
his mission did he speak of his earlier life, the
life of Nazareth. That private life remains secret, totally hidden. What changed him then?
How did his vocation begin? All we know is
that in later life he saw no contradiction between his old life and the exercise of his new
mission.

In point of fact, Jesus never really explained
just who he was. He left the Jews, the masses,
and even his own disciples in doubt. Demons
denounced him and he commanded the demons
to be still (Mark 2:12). When the multitudes
acclaimed him as Messiah, he fled from them.
John the Baptist was perplexed about him and
asked him through his disciples, "Are you the
one who is to come or have we got to look for

someone else?" In reply Jesus said to them, "Go back and tell John what you hear and see; the blind see again, and the lame walk, lepers are cleansed, the deaf hear . . . " (Matthew 11:3–4). But that was all he said.

When Peter, responding to the question of Jesus, said to him: "You are the Christ" (Mark 8:29), Jesus "gave them strict orders not to tell anyone" (Mark 8:30).

We have nothing to help us substantially in imagining Jesus' own consciousness in these circumstances. Nevertheless, no one during all the time of his earthly life seems to have suspected he was more than a man. They knew well that he was extraordinary. His disciples believed that the things he did and the words he said came from God and they qualified him as a person invested with a divine mission. The coming of the Messiah was present in the consciousness of all the Jewish people. Could he be the Messiah? Certainly his followers asked themselves that. But no one suspected he could be something more. That "something more" was well hidden. In fact, in all the conduct referred to by the evangelists (except by John, who many times projects in the gospel the things he discovered after the resurrection), nothing about Jesus hinted he might be some-one whose nature was different from that of other people. Without doubt, Jesus was a man who stood out from his contemporaries. But he was only a man.

We must not be too quick to condemn the "lack of faith" or the "blindness" of his contem-poraries and even of his disciples. Is it not better to respect the anonymity in which God clothed Jesus? If God had wanted his particular presence in the man Jesus to remain hidden, he had a motive. There is no special reason for us to raise this question here. Might it not be that we too need to accompany the human Jesus during a long journey, as if a divine person were not in him, instead of wanting to penetrate at once the secret of his divinity? Might it not be that God wants to show us that if we do not make this long journey of understanding the humanity of Jesus we will forfeit the discovery of his true divinity and discover in its place an idol of our own making?

It is significant that Jesus never promoted, suggested, nor accepted any form, gesture, or word of cult directed to him alone. The disciples treated him with respect, at times with fear, but never with adoration or with religious awe. They accepted him as prophet, wonder worker, or a Messiah, but never as a God. It was only much later, above all when the message of Paul took Christianity to the pagan lands, especially in Asia, that communities born in the midst of the oriental cults created a liturgy in honor of Jesus Christ. It was they who made the cult of Jesus, and made the words "Christian" mean to the eyes of the world "one practicing the cult of Jesus." There were those who practiced the cult of Sarapis, others that of Attis, others that of Mithra, others that of Christ. We, however, are not able to accept at once this definition of being a Christian. The gospels teach us that what Jesus wanted above all were disciples who would accompany him and continue his mission and live their lives according to their own best understanding of his teachings, not people who would simply practice his cult. The cult of Jesus is legitimate. However, it needs to be moderated to include that passage by which his disciples discovered Jesus simply as man, prescinding from his divine quality. During a good part of the way, we need to accept and respect the anonymity of God and to pay attention to the fact that Jesus is really man, to hear him, and to accompany him as if we were accompanying a man.

## HIS LONELINESS

What stands out most, in the first place, in the picture of Jesus is his aloneness. We have already seen his distance from his family. In his own life he practiced the demand imposed on the disciples: "Anyone who prefers father or mother to me is not worthy of me. Anyone who prefers son or daughter is not worthy of me" (Matthew 10:37). He summed up discipleship in this way: "All who abandon houses or brothers or sisters or father or sons or farms for love of my name . . . receive a hundred fold." And he could say this because he did it first himself.

Free of family, he remained alone. He had neither wife nor children. He never clung to any of the companions of his youth, his colleagues, the friends with whom he talked at the doors of the towns he passed. He did not enter into any party, nor any faction. He was not an Essene, nor a Pharisee. He would not let himself be classified. He was a solitary man.

When he withdrew to pray in a desert place, he was alone (Mark 1:35). It is not strange that the three disciples left him in solitary prayer in Gethsemane (Mark 14:32–43). It had always been so. Between him and the disciples he chose the relationship always was, in a certain way, unilateral or unequal. He was always the teacher and they were the students. True friendship with him never took the form of camaraderie, and thus it did not exclude loneliness.

By a reflection he makes on the occasion of the coming of Jesus to Jerusalem, John illustrates this loneliness: "But Jesus knew them all and did not trust himself to them; he never needed evidence about any man; he could tell what a man had in him" (John 2:24–25). This kind of intuition inevitably isolates one.

The gospels show that ever since the day he felt himself called from Galilee to the Jordan where John baptized, Jesus did not belong to himself anymore. He was entirely devoured by his mission. He did not even have a fixed abode. "Foxes have holes and the birds of the air have nests, but the Son of Man has nowhere to lay his head" (Matthew 8:20). He never lingered long in one place. When the disciples looked for him, he responded: "Let us go elsewhere, to the neighboring country towns, so that I can preach there too, because that is why I came" (Mark 1:38).

From this came further loneliness. Others stayed behind preoccupied by a thousand things. Only Jesus went on without stopping, always driven by the vision of the mission which awaited him. No one could share this preoccupation with him to such a point.

Lonely in life and lonely in death, Jesus lived surrounded by people. He was almost never physically alone. He kept few hours for himself, yet he was lonely in the midst of friends and of enemies who rarely left him to himself. His life was not in any way like the life of a monk who lives secluded in a monastery. In the midst of a crowd, he evangelized during the years of his public life; in the midst of a crowd, he died on the cross.

Nevertheless, he did not seem to feel ill at ease among people. He did not practice any kind of cult of loneliness. It was simply his way of life. He had no illusions about people, but never did he look down on them. He sometimes spoke harsh, indignant, passionate, or cruel words, but never words of contempt. He insulted the Pharisees, his adversaries, without despising them at all.

## HIS FRIENDS

The loneliness of Jesus was not insensibility. He never exhibited the kind of psychological tension which so often afflicts religious leaders. He was never distant, aloof, unreachable as certain important people, immersed in their responsibilities, so often are. He did not brush off the importunate with an air of someone in a hurry, with a thousand things to do. In his relationship with people he always acted like the simple artisan he was, treating their problems one by one. He did not synthesize, plan, or organize. He treated everyone he met as a friend—or enemy—but always as a concrete person.

Jesus had friends. The sacred texts preserve the memory of episodes of his friendships. There were the women who sacrificed themselves to care for his material life, and whom the gospel discreetly mentions without comment. "With him went the twelve, as well as certain women who had been cured of evil spirits and ailments: Mary surnamed the Magdalene, from whom seven demons had gone out, Joanna, the wife of Herod's steward Chuza, Susanna, and several others who were providing for them out of their own resources" (Luke 8:2-3).

Mary, Martha, and Lazarus are friends whom readers of the New Testament encounter in the very brief episode of Luke 38:42, and in the long narration of the resurrection of Lazarus in John's gospel. Even so, their friendship stays subordinated to the mission of Jesus. The evangelists give us to understand that the visits were motivated by his apostolate. There is no division in the life of Jesus. Everything he did was done to further the message which he felt he had to proclaim.

His disciples too were his friends. "I call you friends" (John 15:15), he told them. However, this friendship was, in a certain sense, a vocation, a task appointed to them, something more than an ordinary human relationship: "You are my friends if you do what I command you" (John 15:14). Such a delicate relationship as that between Jesus and the disciples invites careful scrutiny.

## HIS DISCIPLES

We have already touched on the unilateral quality of the relationship between Jesus and the Twelve. He himself insisted on this fact: "You have not chosen me, but I have chosen you" (John 15:16). Given this condition, it is very evident why the gospels see no value in their "interpersonal" relations or in the psychology of friendship. The relationship of Jesus with his disciples can be understood only in the context of his mission. Jesus did not concern himself with the families of his disciples or with the families of friends or colleagues. "Another disciple said to him: 'Lord let me go first and bury my father.' But Jesus told him, 'Follow me and let the dead bury the dead' " (Matthew 8:21–22).

The evangelical recollections of the relationship of Jesus to his disciples are placed under the sign of two episodes: their choice by him and their mission. In the gospels, we do not encounter anything that resembles particular conversations, such as the followers of Saint Francis record in the "Fioretti."

The choice of the disciples already looks forward to their future mission: "As he was walking along by the Sea of Galilee, he saw Simon and his brother Andrew casting a net into the lake—they were fishermen. And Jesus said to them, 'Follow me and I will make you into fishers of men.' And at once they left their nets and followed him" (Mark 1:16–18).

The second stage came later: "He made a tour round the villages, teaching. Then he summoned the Twelve and began to send them out in pairs, giving them authority over the unclean spirits" (Mark 6:7–8).

The primacy of the mission must not, however, be interpreted in terms of a purely utilitarian relationship. Out of the disciples' common life and their service of a common goal was born a profound organization and a genuine attachment to Jesus and each other, based on a truly human insight: The disciples were not the servant-priests of the cult of their God or workers at the service of a company to conquer souls; they were collaborators and real friends of Jesus. Unless we realize this, we can never really comprehend the fidelity of the disciples, for example, in the hour of danger when Jesus was called to Bethany: "Then Thomas—known as the Twin—said to the other disciples, 'Let us go too, and die with him' " (John 11:16). Even the fact that this fidelity did not hold fast at the hour of its trial does not belie the intention of the apostles. The sacrifices they accepted show the affection they had for Jesus. As Peter said, "We have left everything and followed you" (Mark 10:28).

And Jesus required radical sacrifices. Even in the hour of uncertainty, when Jesus asked the Twelve, "What about you, do you want to go away too?" Simon Peter answered, "Lord, whom shall we go to? You have the message of eternal life, and we believe; we know that you are the Holy One of God" (John 6:67–68).

There was, however, always an area of incommunicability between the teacher and his followers. Jesus was never able to make them understand the most disconcerting aspect of his mission—his precipitous march to death. Not that this is too surprising. We can easily assume that this will always be the obstacle between Christ and the Christian—the scandal of the cross. Jesus revealed it to his own disciples only gradually, first keeping silent about it and refraining from communicating his feeling of imminent and inescapable death. When much later he began to tell it to his friends, Peter took him aside and began to remonstrate with him. At this Jesus turned around and, eyeing the disciples, reprimanded Peter: "Get behind me, Satan! Because the way you think is not God's way but man's!" (Mark 8:32–33).

The disciples' incomprehension extended also to other aspects of his mission. While waiting for the end, Jesus remained open and at the disposal of a kingdom which was totally in the hands of God. This was an unforeseen, imponderable, inscrutable kingdom, even though the disciples made speculations about it, as ecclesiastics in all times have always made kingdoms their own business and attempted to organize them: "At this time the disciples came to Jesus and said, 'Who is greatest in the kingdom of heaven?' " (Matthew 18:1). Another time, "James and John, the sons of Zebedee, approached him. 'Master,' they said to him, 'we want you to do us a favor.' He said to them, 'What is it you want me to do for you?' They said to him, 'Allow us to sit one at your right hand and the other at your left in your glory' " (Mark 10:35–37).

The area of incommunicability between Jesus and those closest to him is illustrated in the context of the Last Supper, when Philip suddenly says to him: " 'Lord, let us see the Father, and then we shall be satisfied.' 'Have I been with you all this time, Philip,' said Jesus to him, 'and you still do not know me? To have seen me is to have seen the Father' " (John 14:8–9).

The distance between Jesus and his disciples

widened in his final days: the betrayal of Judas, which was a scandal to his colleagues who, apparently, did not expect it; the flight of the disciples in Gethsemane; the denial of Peter—all seem to put the solidity of the disciples' relationship to their Master in question. Still we are not able to conclude that living together during these three years was a failure. The real lesson to be learned here is not one of the collapse, but of the fragility of the disciples' commitment. And even in spite of this, we have a very clear demonstration later on of how valuable that living together was. There is simply no comparison between the weakness of the apostles before the resurrection and the force of their faith afterward. If this faith did not exist during Jesus' public life, the lives of the disciples would have nothing to teach us, and we would have to seek our inspiration in the faith of the early Christian communities. Further, this would mean we could put from our minds the hard fact that the resurrection of Christ does not take weakness from us. We, as much as the apostles, are in danger of falling into the temptation of infidelity. The apostles' weakness in no way lessens the value of the imperfect learning of the Master's teaching.

## HIS AUDIENCE

Jesus attracted crowds. When the people had learned of the many marvelous cures he performed, they rushed to him. Just as today, when the fame of a wonder worker is spread abroad, crowds come running, and millions and millions of miserable humans, usually hidden, emerge into the daylight. Jesus did not deny himself to the crowd that assembled thus. He taught them. He did not reserve his teaching to a privileged group. He spoke to all, openly and publicly, in accord with his parables, that of the sower and the seed, for example (Mark 1:28,32–35; 2:1–11).

"Jesus withdrew from his disciples to the lakeside, and great crowds from Galilee followed him. From Judaea, Jerusalem, Idumaea, Transjordania, and the region of Tyre and Sidon, great numbers who had heard of all he was doing came to him. And he asked his disciples to have a boat ready for him because of the crowd, to keep him from being crushed. For he had cured so many that all who were afflicted in any way were crowding forward to touch him" (Mark 3:7–10). On another occasion, when he began to teach beside a lake, such a huge crowd gathered around him, that he went and sat in a boat on the water, while the crowd remained on the nearby shore (Mark 4:1).

Never, however, did Jesus join the multitude for very long. He neither organized it, nor proposed forms of action to it. He spoke, and he went his way.

In the same way, in Jerusalem, he taught many times publicly in the temple, but did not attempt to gather the fruits of his discourses. He was able to apply to himself what he said to his followers: "One sows, another reaps. I sent you to reap a harvest you have not worked for. Others worked for it and you have come into the rewards of their trouble" (John 4:37–38).

Throughout his ministry, Jesus showed himself to everyone. In a short time, he made himself a very public person. He became the center of debate, an object of passionate controversy. Far from avoiding publicity, he actively encouraged it. Thus, he lived accompanied by a crowd, which renewed itself without ceasing, and left him almost no tranquility. After a while, he even aroused unrest in the public officials; Herod, the elders, the priests, the scribes, and Pilate took fright. Jesus was able to declare in perfect truth to Caiaphas have spoken openly for all the world to hear; I have always taught in a synagogue or in the temple where all the Jews meet together. I have said nothing secret. But why ask me? Ask my hearers what I have taught; they know what I said" (John 18:20–21).

Jesus died abandoned, solitary, but among the multitude of his people, in front of the authorities who condemned him. His human career terminated in question: Who was he? Why had this man so strange a destiny? From the beginning until the end, a continuous line appeared: a mission which absorbed the man but never destroyed any of the humanity in him. Jesus never acted like a machine. He lived as if pulled by destiny to the testimony of his death. This awful attraction did not make him flee far from people or pass the three years which separated him from death in a kind of "retreat" of preparation. He made his "retreat" before the masses, in the midst of a group of disciples who almost never left him alone.

Such is all of the man that we can know. For us, he is twice a foreigner, difficult to understand. Foreigner, first of all, because he was Jewish, and his gestures and words never lose for us a certain tone of the exotic. We know full well how much this foreignness favors a certain drifting into myth. Though it is difficult to mythologize persons near to us and too well known, a certain strangeness creates the mystery favorable to a mythologization. But despite all this, the evangelical text cannot be a pretext for the easy fixing of a conventional picture, like those images which represent Jesus in the conventional dress of his time, with long hair and face quasi-feminine style; this stylized "Jesus" is born of an exoticism far too routine and recognizable. It falsifies his real humanity, substituting instead a conventional symbol (the image, for example, of the Sacred Heart). Though some unthinking persons probably find satisfaction in that symbol, it divests Jesus of his historical reality. Jesus is really accessible only when we make the effort to translate the Judaic figure into the language of our present culture. If we do not, we fall into myth.

There is a second way that Jesus can be foreign to us. He belongs to a pre-technical epoch, with oral culture and artisan economists. Today's peasant-farmers can still identify with him. But the rest of us, who have already passed through the modern schools, need to recover our pre-technical souls to understand. The pride of technical development often hides reality and leads people to be confused by cultural facts belonging to a prior era. We must translate them to our times, and try to understand. The wisdom of Jesus is not improved by contact with modern science and technology. It is from another epoch, and the barrier of archaic culture can make it difficult for us to understand.

## CHAPTER II

# *Freedom*

## A FREE PEOPLE

It must be remembered that, above all, Jesus was a free man. His liberty shone in the face of his adversaries. His example emancipated the consciousness of his disciples and threatened the power of those who wanted to keep them captive. After barely three years of public life, Jesus died because he did not want to hide or lessen in the least the exterior manifestations of his liberty. He died because he threatened the prudence and the wisdom of the powerful who felt challenged by his liberty. This liberty was not merely a trait of character, a distinctive sign of his personality. It was much more. Jesus showed himself as a free man because liberation and liberty were the nucleus of his message. Paul condenses this message in a few words:

37

"My brothers, you were called, as you know, to liberty" (Galatians 5:13).

Still, Jesus did not invent this aspiration to liberty, this pervasive atmosphere of freedom. He encountered it in the bosom of his people. He knew the soul of his people and wanted to penetrate it deeply. He wanted to reach into the soul of the people of Israel and awaken its deepest part to a perspective more radical than any Israelite had done before him.

The Jews said of themselves with pride: "We are descendants from Abraham, and never have we been slaves to anyone" (John 8:33–34). By this they meant that they had never accepted their slavery: the slavery of Egypt or the slavery of Babylon, the servitude to kings who defeated them and treated them as chattel. Never in their history had they conformed to this condition or accepted it as an inevitable destiny.

God was the liberator of Israel from the time of the slavery of Egypt. Moses, whom God sent as a guide and liberator (Acts 7:35), said to the sons of Israel: "God will raise up a prophet like myself for you from among your own brothers" (Acts 7:37). For Stephen the proto-martyr, who quotes these ancient words, there is no doubt that this prophet, this new liberation, is Jesus himself. Isaiah announced the renewal of the liberation from Egypt with the promise of a new exodus, and the disciples recognized that these promises corresponded to the work of Jesus and to his way of life. Through his behavior, the Jewish people spontaneously identified Jesus with the Messiah, that is, with him from whom the hope of a new liberation sprang. Jesus did not respond as expected to the people's demands, nor did he admit to be the kind of liberator they awaited. He did not want the rumor that the Messiah had arrived to spread. Still, alone with his disciples, he accepted Peter's identification of him as the Awaited One (Mark 8:29). The dreams of the disciples at Emmaus were not vain ones: "Our own hope had been that he would be the one to set Israel free" (Luke 24:21). Jesus responded to their hopes, but in another way. In any case, to understand the life of Jesus, the scripture reader must also understand that he entered into his ministry in a world preoccupied with liberty. Jesus was born, he grew up, he became himself in the midst of a people so concerned, and he received from them his sense of liberty. His consciousness of his calling was developed in relation to the anxieties and the aspirations of a people who had waited a long time to be free.

Other nations lived conformed and resigned to their fates. It is impossible to conceive of Jesus being born in a family of slaves in Rome, in a tribe in which conformity overwhelmed individual initiative, or in a family of oppressors. Historically, he could have been born only in Israel. Only a nation where the people were poor but proud, beaten and exploited but never really submissive, could have produced him.

It is true that at the time Jesus appeared the Roman domination tended to exacerbate Israel's desire for national independence. But this is merely one aspect (and not the basic one) of the question of liberty. Independence does not immediately produce liberty. One foreign dominator can always be succeeded by another, no better than the one before. We know that Jesus never sympathized with the movements of the Jewish guerrillas who thought they could win their independence by means of armed revolt and who reduced the problem of liberty to the autonomy of their own people. He did not sympathize with them because his preoccupation with liberty was not limited to his own compatriots. It extended to all nations. The armed revolt of Israel was not the best way to spread his message within the Roman empire proper. On the contrary, such action would have closed the door to it entirely.

The roots of liberty are more profound and are not established simply by the conquest of political power. Even if one day it does include political power, true liberty advances in other ways. Certainly, Jesus, like the majority of his contemporaries, had sense enough to understand that the Roman empire, then at the peak of its power, was so strong that any attempt at revolt, similar to that of the Zealots, was condemned to failure.

In any case, the Old Testament already had made clear that the liberty of Israel did not refer simply to its relation with other nations or rest purely on the level of international politics. Liberty was and should be a way of life, a form of collective and personal existence of a different quality. To be free does not necessarily mean to be independent. It means to live according to the mode of liberty. And what is this mode? The history and the fundamental documents of Israel reveal it to us.

The people of Israel were not the property of anyone: They belonged to God alone. In this

case, therefore, there could be neither
dominators nor dominated. All were members
of the same alliance. And the alliance was not
only a pact between God and man; it was also a
pact in which men were joined to God and to
each other. The Covenant was the first sugges-
tion in the history of humanity of a people
brought together by a contract accepted voluntarily. When it was celebrated on Mount Sinai,
God said: "I will count you a kingdom of
priests, a consecrated nation" (Exodus 19:6).
(So, at least the early Christians understood the
testimony of the book of Apocalypse.) God
meant the Israelites to be no man's servants. All
would be kings and priests; all would be equal.
The difference among them lay only in the
division of labor that the book of Deuteronomy
describes. The mission of Jesus, therefore,
must be situated in the framework of the promise of a people of kings and priests—a people of
brothers and sisters, united by the same pact
and alliance of familyhood, equal and respect-
ful one of the other, according to the spirit of
the Law.

In a word, not only was Jesus born among a
people to whom liberty had been, from their
beginning, the touchstone of national life, but

he situated his mission within the boundary of this principal focal point. From this base he saw the vocation of his people. This is what we shall now examine in his acts and in his words.

## INDEPENDENCE

Jesus lived free. We already know he did not depend on his family. The single episode in the gospel which refers to the course of his life in Nazareth shows us an adolescent already conscious of the independence in which his vocation placed him. Jesus did not bind himself to any association or party. He did not submit himself to a synagogue, as was the practice among the Jews. He was not enrolled in one of the schools where the scribes got their degrees. He never knew the worry associated with acquiring a diploma. He was not a landowner and consequently never needed the support of the law or the police to defend his property.

Jesus asked nothing of the rich or those in power: neither license, nor approval, nor collaboration. He did not need them. Without doubt, this is where he hurt them the most: He showed he did not need them. He visited the rich, the Pharisees, the influential, without ever asking for help. He received a man as important as Nicodemus without asking him for his approval, his intervention with authority, even for a friendly word in the Sanhedrin. He must have known that if so influential a person as Nicodemus guaranteed his good conduct in the assembly, it would be considered a powerful argument for his cause. The rich know how to forgive many offenses, if one comes to ask for money or for recommendation from them. Jesus did not look for this.

Pilate, too, was surprised by Jesus' independence. He certainly hoped the prisoner would appeal to his clemency. It would have given him the opportunity to show his power. Everything that happened indicates that a sufficiently humble petition from Jesus would have been enough to satisfy the vanity of the Roman representative. "Are you refusing to speak to me? Surely you know I have power to release you and to crucify you" (John 19:10). But Jesus remained inflexible. Any one else probably would have given in; but Jesus did not take one step to facilitate the proceedings, to help in the sense of making peace with them. No word to disarm the Jews, no word to placate Pilate. From the beginning of his life until its end,

Jesus did not ask anything for himself of anyone. No one could boast that Jesus had asked for life or even tranquility from him. He was inflexible, without arrogance, but irreducibly inflexible. This characteristic so profoundly marked the first Christians that one can see it in the answers that the martyrs gave when they stood before their Roman judges.

## THE LIBERATION OF ISRAEL

If we want to understand the meaning of liberty and especially the liberty of Jesus, we must place it in the context of the world of Israel. "If you make my word your home you will indeed be my disciples; you will learn the truth and the truth will make you free" (John 8:31–32). But this could have many different meanings. There were times when, inspired by the culture and by the philosophy of the past, readers imagined Jesus as a philosopher distant from the agitations of the exterior world, preoccupied with the interior life, for whom the problem of liberty was (much as for the philosopher-slave Epictetus) only a problem of interior liberty. The slave was free who was able to maintain his autonomy in the deepest part of his consciousness. True, Jesus was preoccupied with the problem of the interior life and that of the conscience of his disciples. He was indeed a moralist and an educator of interior lives. But he was not a philosopher, and he did not understand liberty as did the philosophers of the Roman world. Jesus was Jewish and understood liberty as did the Jews.

Free people were all around him. He already had them to speak to—crowds made up of the poor of Israel and formed in the spirit of the prophets. He did not have to stimulate them. They (the remnant of true Israel) could be emissaries, the missionaries of liberty to the entire world. What then was left for him to do with them? Nothing more or less than to teach these poor of Israel to protect and guarantee their liberty from the threats, the seduction, and the false education of their bad pastors, the religious leaders who attempted to mislead them. Free people were there, but they had been seduced, maintained in a false slavery through false interpretations by the Pharisees, the priests, and the scribes.

This is the context in which we must understand the conflict of Jesus with the Pharisees and the scribes. Jesus did not need to form a

free people. They were already formed. The
only thing they still lacked was an understanding of the vanity, the insanity, and the falsity of
the pseudo-Israel which was taught them by
the corruptors of their traditions. Jesus set out
to destroy this false power over them and to
liberate the conscience of the simple from er-
roneous veneration of their leaders in order to
reconstruct the true face, the true image of the
people of God. Liberty was present in the tradition of Israel as the inexhaustible deposit of the
free spirit of many centuries. False guides had
kept these reserves turned off and unused. It
was necessary to awaken a people put to sleep
by bad counselors and paralyzed by a religion
of precepts and works, of fear and rigor, which
completely took from them the spirit of liberty
and the realization of its universality. Jesus
planned his combat on that central point. He
set out to restore the people of God to themselves, returning to them the sense of their own
value and the divine energies God gave them.
The people would do the rest.

If Jesus had been a Roman philosopher, we
would think it typical that he did not treat of the
problem of the city and the empire, or of moral
virtues on the social level. He would seem to us

a philosopher of the interior, personal life. He would be the Jesus of Renan—who, curiously, is also the Jesus of so many Catholics. But Jesus was no Roman philosopher. If he did not bother with the social and political problems of the city and the empire, it was not because these things were unimportant to the kingdom of God, but because he knew the people themselves would naturally resolve these concerns. It was not necessary to define the revolutions of the future; the people would take care of that. Jesus did not come to *substitute* for the people of God; nor did he come to furnish them with a social, political, or military leader. He came only to liberate them from fear and from the false religious submission in which the Pharisees kept them. Once rid of these misconceptions, the free people educated in the tradition of the Old Testament would do the rest—as indeed they did do, or at least begin to in the twenty centuries which separate us from his message. Jesus did not fight against the economic, social, or political systems of his time. He simply freed his people from the adversary who kept them slaves within themselves.

From this, we can see why Jesus left the

priests and ancients in peace. They had neither influence nor prestige in the eyes of the people. Since they were already powerless, it was unnecessary to disturb them. But the Pharisees were pious and religious, and the fame of their sanctity was great. They claimed to be the authentic interpreters of the law of Israel. They were the real threat and the danger, the great corruptors of that Israel of which they judged themselves the purest guides and defenders. The liberation of Israel from the yoke of these scribes and Pharisees, the restoration of its soul to the impetus of the Spirit of God, was the task to which Jesus consecrated the major part of his work.

But how to fight this false religion of the scribes and Pharisees? First Jesus had to show that he was personally free of it and make solemn and clear gestures of rejection and condemnation of this kind of religion. Here we find the element of provocation in the attitude of Jesus in the face of the law as interpreted by the Pharisees. Instead of looking for conciliation, Jesus actually sought confrontation. It was in that spirit he said to the disciples: "I have come to set a man against his father, a daughter against her mother, a daughter-in-law against her mother-in-law. A man's enemies will be those of his own household" (Matthew 10:35–36).

Jesus provoked this confrontation by questioning the works of piety and the air of sanctity of the scribes and Pharisees. He himself did not have an "air of sanctity." Nor did he have the "face of a saint." In fact, his enemies reacted to him with this accusation: "Look, a glutton and drunkard, a friend of tax collectors and sinners" (Matthew 11:19). "When John's disciples and the Pharisees were fasting, some people came and said to him, 'Why is it that John's disciples and the disciples of the Pharisees fast, but your disciples do not?' " (Mark 2:18). And Jesus responded to them: "Surely the bridegroom's attendants would never think of fasting while the bridegroom is with them? As long as they have the bridegroom with them, they could not think of fasting" (Mark 2:19).

Following this principle, Jesus liberated himself, as well as his followers, from the religious restrictions by which the scribes kept people prisoners.

One sabbath day, he happened to be taking a walk through the cornfields, and his disciples began to pick ears of corn as they went along and the

Pharisees said to him, "Look, why are they doing something on the sabbath day that is forbidden?" And he replied, "Did you never read what David did in his time of need when he and his followers were hungry—how he went into the house of God when Abiathar was high priest, and ate the loaves of offering which only the priests are allowed to eat, and how he also gave some to the men with him?" And he said to them, "The sabbath was made for man, not man for the sabbath: So the Son of Man is master even of the sabbath" (Mark 2:23–28).

And again:

He went into a synagogue, and there was a man there who had a withered hand. And they were watching him to see if he would cure him on the sabbath day, hoping for something to use against him. He said to the man with the withered hand, "Stand up out in the middle!" Then he said to them, "Is it against the law on the sabbath day to do good, or to do evil; to save life, or to kill?" But they said nothing. Then, grieved to find them so obstinate, he looked angrily around at them, and said to the man, "Stretch out your hand." He stretched it out and his hand was better. The Pharisees went out and at once began to plot with the Herodians against him, discussing how to destroy him (Mark 3:1–6).

It is very clear that Jesus could have avoided this conflict. He could have cured this cripple on the day before the sabbath or the day after.

But he wanted the conflict to free his followers from the fear of the law and its interpreters.

Another criterion used by his enemies for selection of "good men" were the rules of purification. "The Pharisees and some of the scribes who had come from Jerusalem gathered around him, and they noticed that some of his disciples were eating with unclean hands, that is, without washing them" (Mark 7:1–2). Luke attributed the disobedience to Jesus himself. "He had just finished speaking when a Pharisee invited him to dine at his house. He went in and sat down at the table. The Pharisee saw this and was surprised that he had not first washed before the meal" (Luke 11:37–39). This was an even greater scandal.

Another confrontation came of Jesus' visiting of public sinners. On the day that he called on Levi, son of Alphaeus, this occurred: "When Jesus was at dinner in his house, a number of tax collectors and sinners were also sitting at the table with Jesus and his disciples; for there were many of them among his followers. When the scribes and the Pharisees saw him eating with sinners and tax collectors, they said to his disciples, 'Why does he eat with tax collectors and sinners?' " (Mark 2:14–16).

One of the Pharisees invited him to a meal. When he arrived at the Pharisee's house and took his place at table, a woman came in, who had a bad name in the town. She had heard he was dining with the Pharisee and had brought with her an alabaster jar of ointment. She waited behind him at his feet, weeping, and her tears fell on his feet, and she wiped them away with her hair; then she covered his feet with kisses and anointed them with the ointment. When the Pharisee who had invited him saw this, he said to himself, "If this man were a prophet, he would know who this woman is that is touching him and what a bad name she has" (Luke 7:36–40).

But Jesus referred his conduct directly to God, and not to the precepts established by human traditions. As such, he created among the disciples a radical criticism of all human institutions, an attitude which much later would provoke a permanent criticism of society.

## CONFLICT

The Pharisees immediately recognized that they were the principal object of Jesus' denunciation—they, the party most "religious" and most faithful in attachment to religion. They tried to submit him to examination according to their own criteria: the knowledge of ecclesiastical law. "Some Pharisees approached him and asked, 'Is it against the law for a man to divorce?' " (Mark 10:2). Much later, "Next day they sent to him some Pharisees and some Herodians to catch him out in what he said. These came and said to him, 'Master we know you are an honest man, that you are not afraid of anyone, because a man's rank means nothing to you, and that you teach the way of God in all honesty. Is it permissible to pay taxes to Caesar or not? Should we pay, yes or no?' " (Mark 12:13–14).

"The Pharisees came up and started a discussion with him; they demanded of him a sign from heaven, to test him. And with a sigh that came straight from the heart he said, 'Why does this generation demand a sign? I tell you solemnly, no sign shall be given to this generation' " (Mark 8:11–12). And he instructed his disciples: "Keep your eyes open; be on guard against the yeast of the Pharisees and the yeast of Herod" (Mark 8:15).

Tradition, as gathered by the first gospel, gives a list of Jesus' denunciations and accusations against them:

The scribes and Pharisees occupy the chair of Moses. You must therefore do what they tell you and listen to what they say. But do not act according to their works; for they talk but do nothing. They tie up heavy burdens and lay them on men's shoulders, but will they lift a finger to move them? Not they! Everything they do is done to attract attention, like wearing broader phylacteries and longer tassels, like wanting to take the place of honor at banquets and the front seats in the synagogues, being greeted obsequiously in the market squares and having people call them "Rabbi" (Matthew 23:2–7).

Alas for you scribes and Pharisees, you hypocrites! You who shut up the kingdom of heaven in men's faces, neither going in yourselves nor admitting others to go in who want to.

Alas for you scribes and Pharisees, you hypocrites! You who travel over sea and land to make a single proselyte, and when you have him, you make him twice as fit for hell as you are.

Alas for you, blind guides! You who say, "If a man swears by the temple, it has no force; but if a man swears by the gold of the temple, he is bound." Fools and blind! For which is of greater worth, the gold or the temple which makes the gold sacred? Or else, "If a man swears by the altar, it has no force; but if a man swears by the offering that is on the altar, he is bound." You blind men! For which is of greater worth, the offering or the altar that makes the offering sacred? Therefore, when a man swears by the altar he is swearing by that and by everything on it. And when a man swears by the temple he is swearing by the throne of God and by the One who is seated there.

Alas for you, scribes and Pharisees, you hypo-

crites! You who pay tithe of mint and dill and cum-
min, and have neglected the weightier matters of the
law—justice, mercy, good faith! These you should
have practiced without neglecting the others. You
blind guides! Straining at gnats and swallowing
camels!

Alas for you, scribes and Pharisees, you hypocrites! You who clean the outside of cup and dish,
and leave the inside full of extortion and intemper-
ance. Blind Pharisees! Clean the inside of cup and
dish first so that the outside may become clean as
well.

Alas for you scribes and Pharisees, you hypocrites! You who are like whitewashed tombs that
look handsome on the outside, but inside are full of
dead men's bones and every kind of corruption.
In the same way you appear to people from the outside like good honest men, but inside you are full
of hypocrisy and lawlessness.

Alas for you, scribes and Pharisees, you hypocrites! You who build the sepulchres of the prophets
and decorate the tombs of holy men, saying, "We
would never have joined in shedding the blood of
the prophets, had we lived in our fathers' day!" So!
your own evidence tells against you! You are the
sons of those who murdered the prophets! Very
well then, finish off the work that your fathers
began (Matthew 23:13–32).

The anathemas of Jesus were not aimed directly against the social authorities, Judaic or

Roman. At first glance it may have seemed only a fight against a religious party, or a particular interpretation of religion. However, the authorities saw very clearly that Jesus' message was not just an opinion of one new rabbinical school among many. They foresaw that his teaching put their whole society in question and they were not disposed to allow such questioning. The Pharisees' scruples about Jesus' behavior did not trouble them particularly, but his position with reference to a proclamation of liberty for the people of Israel constituted a threat and worried the authorities. Though Jesus never performed an act of insurrection, at the same time he refused any conciliation with the authorities. He left them as he found them.

He practiced perfect liberty in the face of the Judaic authorities: "They came to Jerusalem again, and as Jesus was walking in the temple, the chief priests and the scribes and the elders came to him, and they said to him, 'What authority have you for acting like this? Or who gave you authority to do these things?' " (Mark 11:27–28). After questioning his questioners about the authority under which John the Baptist acted, Jesus concluded, "Nor will I tell you my authority for acting like this" (Mark 11:33).

Pilate asked Jesus a similar question: "Where do you come from?" (John 19:9). Just as the chiefs of the Jews, Pilate wanted to examine Jesus' credentials for acting as he did. "Jesus made no answer." Pilate then said to him: "Are you refusing to speak? Surely you know I have power to release you and I have power to crucify you?" (John 9:9–11). Pilate wanted to be the judge and Jesus did not accept the role of the one judged, although he had nothing against Pilate personally, or against the way Pilate exercised the power he had received.

Jesus' total independence made death unavoidable for him. He refused to sacrifice his liberty; he refused to make concessions. He was a conscious and deliberate victim of his radicalism. The way the world works is that the only way a man can save himself is by agreeing to compromise and to accept accommodations with the forces in power.

However, in the short view and the long, it was this very intransigence taught and lived by Jesus that held the disciples together as a group and saved the future Church. The disciples were able to see the radical opposition between the established Jewish system and the rule of God over Israel: "This man who was put into your power by the deliberate intention and foreknowledge of God, you took and had crucified by men outside the Law. You killed him, but God raised him to life, freeing him from the pangs of Hades, for it was impossible for him to be held in its power" (Acts 2:23–25). "The God of Abraham, of Isaac, and of Jacob, the God of our ancestors, has glorified his servant Jesus, the same Jesus you handed over and then disowned in the presence of Pilate after Pilate had decided to release him. It was you who disowned the Holy One, the Just One, you who demanded the reprieve of a murderer while you killed the prince of life. God, however, raised him from the dead" (Acts 3:13–15).

The radicalism of Jesus freed the disciples from the fear, the shame, the timidity, and the false respect of the constituted authorities. It made them capable of formal disobedience: "We cannot promise to stop proclaiming what we have seen and heard" (Acts 4:20).

## SECURITY

Jesus preached liberty and liberated his followers from the yoke of religious and other laws in order to announce the fulfillment of the covenant which God had made with Israel. He was able to preach liberty because he did not know sin. "Can any one of you convict me of sin?" (John 8:46). It is clear that it was not because of the efficacy of the law and the religious system maintained by the pious Israelites that he was sinless. His impeccability was the fruit of the grace of the Spirit he received so abundantly. With him was inaugurated the time in which good and virtue would be the fruit, not of a vain system of practices and of precepts, but of the Spirit. This was to be the permanent challenge of the church: to trust sufficiently in the Spirit to dispense with the resources of systems, of laws, and of rules. How then must the church liberate itself again and again from new rules reappearing after every movement of the Spirit? Herein lies the drama in the history of the church. It appears already written in the life and destiny of Jesus: The passage from a legalistic Old Testament life to an organically-growing New Testament one is the permanent challenge of the Christian church.

Jesus was interiorly and personally free because he was unselfish. He himself was not preoccupied with the future of his life or with

the future of his work. He was free of any form
of anxiety about the future of the kingdom of
God he announced. There has never been
another founder who left to his successors a
work so free, flexible, and non-institutionalized
as Jesus did. To the apostles he left the mission
of continuing what he had begun. He left prac-
tically none of the present institutions of the
Christian Church, except the instruction to
reunite themselves at times, to have a supper
commemorating his death and future coming.
The rest was totally open. He trusted in the
Spirit given to the apostles to define the rites; he
left a church without preoccupying himself
with what would happen to it when it became
threatened. He sowed the seed, but he built
nothing. Never in the gospels did he seem to
worry about what came after him; never did he
say to the apostles: after me, do this or that.
Above all, he himself lived the counsels given to
his disciples: "So do not worry about tomorrow; tomorrow will take care of itself. Each day
has enough troubles of its own" (Matthew
6:34).

He knew that preoccupation with the
future—the need of constructing some kind of
security for themselves—is what oppresses

people. For the common man, security consists in the titles and the guarantees he accumulates for the future—his property, diploma, prestige, esteem, power to confer favors, etc. Jesus did not need approval from his benefactors, because he did not leave them anything, any earthly security. His security was confidence in his mission and in the Spirit he knew the Father would send his followers.

Jesus had no career for which to prepare. From the beginning, he placed himself quite outside all hierarchies. He had decided he would be himself and nothing but himself without taking into account those career comparisons which give value (or non-value) to a person. Free of any careerism, of any wish for promotion or the need of guaranteeing the future, he was able to live as the birds of the air do: "They do not sow or reap, or gather into barns" (Matthew 6:26).

Finally, Jesus overcame the fear of death. He had to confront this fear, and the gospels do not hide the battle that this prospect represented for him. They do not show us an insensible celestial creature. For all of us, death is an uncomfortable and tragic presence, always present as a possible danger, always an object of an irrepressible terror, even if it be only in the constant effort to repress the fear. The danger of death is what leads to concessions, accommodations, silence, lack of participation, and betrayal by those who fall into its shadow. In Jesus' case, danger of death was present from the beginning to the end.

At the same time he took along with him Peter, James, and John. Then he began to be filled with fear and distress. He said to them, "My soul is sorrowful to the point of death. Wait here, and keep awake." And going on a little further he threw himself on the ground and prayed that, if it were possible, this hour might pass him by. "Abba, Father!" he said, "Everything is possible for you. Take this cup away from me. But let it be as you, not I, would have it" (Mark 14:33–37).

This surrender of himself constituted the supreme act of the liberty of Jesus. For three years he constantly confronted death and overcame the temptation: "One who has been tempted in every way we are" (Hebrews 4:15). He knew terror before the prospect of death: "During his life on earth, he offered up prayer and entreaty, aloud and in silent tears, to the one who had the power to save him out of death" (Hebrews 5:7). He overcame temptation and remained free in the face of death.

# CHAPTER III

# *Brotherhood*

## BROTHER AMONG BROTHERS

"I tell you solemnly, in so far as you did this to one of the least of my brothers, you did it to me" (Matthew 25:40). The king who spoke in such a manner was Jesus. He was the brother of all, brother to such a point that he claimed identification with everyone who hungered or thirsted, with whoever was a stranger, who was naked or imprisoned, no matter how miserable and abandoned that person might be. Nothing at all in the gospels stands out more vividly than the exercise of this open and unlimited brotherhood. Referring to those who followed him, Jesus responded one day to the people who brought him a petition from his blood relatives, "Here are my mother and my brothers" (Mark 3:34). His three-year mission was exploited, day after day, by his innumerable brothers.

## THE CROWDS

The brotherhood of Jesus was active service. It did not stop with feelings or with declarations. It was not a passive disposition—simple suffering with his own; it was first of all activity. The way he took to concretize this love is quite extraordinary. Living as he did in a rural and pre-technical civilization, much the same as the setting in which the poor rural masses live today, the major problem, the most intense, most common suffering that he saw was sickness. Health was, in his world, as in that of the modern poor, a constant preoccupation. All the farmers of Brazil say the same thing, if they are asked what is their greatest happiness. Their biggest religious preoccupation is health; almost all their votive promises refer to health. Their pilgrimages rarely have another goal. The prayers they say refer to health. If you see one of them recollected with a quasi-mystical intensity, contemplating the image of a saint, you can be certain he came to ask for or to give thanks for the gift of health for himself or for one of his relatives. So also were the people whom Jesus knew: There was sickness in all families, in all the surrounding neighborhoods —and sickness almost without recourse, without hope.

Even now, in Brazil's rural civilization, there are healers who combine the use of prayer with the knowledge of empirical traditional prescriptions. Some of these healers live as saints, dedicated entirely to the alleviating of the sufferings of others. Some are true mystics, to whom the exercise of healing is a true, holy mission in the name of God and with supernatural powers. Even today, in the interior of Brazil there are healers of this type. Though some take advantage of the credulity of the sufferers, others are authentic saints who practice a heroic love. There are also among them missionaries revered for sanctity, to whom the people attribute numerous miracles. It may well be they really do work miracles. However, it is difficult to separate the powers of faith, confidence, the use of still-unknown psychological energies, and empirical remedies from the exceptional intervention of God.

It may be that all these things are mixed together in these happenings attested to by a credulous, pious, and sincere people.

In any case, the appearance of a great wonder worker was not a fact totally incomprehensible, isolated, or unique in Jesus' time. In the world of healers, the arrival of a wonder worker caused no shock. It was a sign of the excellence of love. The best service one could give a people was to cure the sick. Jesus chose this service. He could give his work no greater sign if he wanted to suggest a really active fraternity and a really attentive God. Jesus was a wonder worker, an extraordinary miracle worker who aroused the enthusiasm of the people, a miracle worker who was greater than the other healers who have left their names behind them.

In his discourse with Cornelius, Peter condensed in a few words the meaning of the sign of the passing of the miracle worker among men: "God had anointed him with the Holy Spirit and power, and because God was with him, Jesus went about doing good works and curing all who had fallen into the power of the devil" (Acts 10:38).

The impression of union with the people stands out well in the conclusions of Matthew:

"He went around the whole of Galilee, teaching in their synagogues, proclaiming the Good News of the kingdom, and curing all kinds of diseases and sickness among the people. His fame spread throughout Syria, and those who were suffering from diseases or complaints of one kind or another, the possessed, epileptics, the paralyzed, were all brought to him and he cured them" (Matthew 4:23–24). Crowds looking for health, often concentrated in certain sanctuaries, are even today the image of an abandoned humanity—this humanity of which Jesus felt himself a brother. "Jesus made a tour through all the towns and villages, teaching in their synagogues, proclaiming the Good News of the kingdom, and curing all kinds of diseases and sickness. And when he saw the crowds he felt sorry for them because they were harrassed and dejected like sheep without a shepherd" (Matthew 9:35–36).

The day at Capernaum (Mark 1:21–39) shows us who came running and who even tried to hold the "saint who does miracles," and how Jesus had to flee from them through the hills of Galilee; however, the people observed him and attempted to discover where he went. Such a thing happened on the day Jesus went off alone after receiving the news of John the Baptist's death. "But the people heard of this, and leaving the towns went after him on foot. So as he stepped ashore, he saw a large crowd, and took pity on them and healed their sick" (Matthew 14:13–14).

After another crossing: "They came to Gennesaret. When the local people recognized him they spread the word through the whole neighborhood and took all that were sick to him, begging him just to let them touch the fringe of his cloak. And all those who touched it were completely cured" (Matthew 14:34–36). "Jesus went on from there and reached the shores of the Sea of Galilee, and he went up into the hills. He sat there and large crowds came to him bringing with them the crippled, the blind, the dumb, and many others; these they put down at his feet and he cured them. The crowds were astonished to see the dumb speaking, the cripples whole again, the lame walking, and the blind with their sight, and they praised the God of Israel" (Matthew 15:29–31).

In these résumés concerning "all the sick" we may expect some exaggeration due to enthusiasm and to the change in perspective created by a distance of forty or fifty years (the

distance between the acts of Jesus and the actual writing of the Gospel of Matthew). We
should also take into account the part played in
the description of the admiration and the credulity of a simple people who had never seen so
many good works, nor known so much hope. In
any event, in Galilee Jesus won the admiration
of the people, but this admiration was contained within a rural world and had little outside social repercussion. For this poor and
abandoned people he was hope at last. They
felt attended to and understood. Perhaps too
much attended. For they wished to make of
him a permanent provider, and that he neither
was, nor could ever be.

We will not attempt to explain "the mercy
miracles" of Jesus historically or scientifically.
Trying to distinguish how much of it to attribute to divine power, to popular credulity, to
the work of psychic forces that we still don't
understand, to the natural gifts of a healer, or to
the creative imagination of the primitive Christian communtities would be a waste of time.
What, at least, is clear is that Jesus gave such
signs of compassion and had such a comprehension of the suffering of the crowds that he was a
true echo of their feelings, and, even today,

awakens the hope of the most miserable. Full of admiration, his contemporaries said: "He has done all things well, he makes the deaf hear and the dumb speak" (Mark 7:37). The surprised people said: "Nothing like this has ever been seen in Israel!" (Matthew 9:34).

This love of Jesus was no impersonal force, no diffusion of a beneficent but anonymous energy. Some gospel stories have transmitted the impression that Jesus had certain special relationships with Martha, Mary, Lazarus, or the "beloved" John. We know very well that tradition stylized these reports. However, what was maintained behind these illustrative mosaic pieces is really the human theme of personal attention. Our problem as Christians of the twentieth century is to find how to save this virtue of personal attention within the context of a complex modern society. Just because Jesus knew only a people of rural and traditional civilization, of small communities having only limited means of communication, does not mean that we should reject his approach.

Since Jesus did not have any social preconception and since he attended to all needs, he responded at once to the plea of the important official, Jairus. He also attended to the petition

of the father of the epileptic child (Mark
9:14–29). He had compassion on the widow of
Naim (Luke 7:11–17). There was no sign there
would not be an answer to any supplication out
of need.

Jesus did not do these signs to convince his
petitioners or to force them to join his followers. The dialogue between Jesus and the
Samaritan woman in the later Gospel of Saint
John only reflects the discussions then in prog-
ress between Christians and Jews in an anti-
Judaic polemic and an apologia for Christ. The
first gospels show the true situation and are
much nearer the facts: Jesus was a miracle
worker and he multiplied good works moved
by the misery of the people and by the supplications which came from them.

## THE SINNERS

The love of Jesus was not an answer to love
received. It was in no way a response. What
was new about it—and he himself had a very
clear consciousness of this newness (Matthew
5:43–45)—was that his was a love which took
the initiative and created love by its own insistence, even in the form of love of enemies. "But

I say this to you: Love your enemies and pray for those who persecute you. . . . For if you love only those who love you, what right have you to claim any credit? Even the tax collectors do as much, do they not? And if you save your greetings for your brothers, are you doing anything exceptional? Even the pagans do as much, do they not?" (Matthew 5:44–48).

The love of enemies supposes pardon of offenses, and gives at the same time a concrete meaning and a material base to this pardon. It is not merely a verbal or sentimental pardon. Jesus commanded us to pray: "And forgive us our debts as we have forgiven those who are in debt to us" (Matthew 6:12). And he further commented: "Yes, if you forgive others their failings your heavenly Father will forgive yours; but if you do not forgive others, your Father will not forgive your failings either" (Matthew 6:14–15).

The parable of the unworthy servant illustrates this doctrine. The master said: " 'You wicked servant, I cancelled all that debt of yours, when you appealed to me. Were you not bound, then, to have pity on your fellow servant, just as I had pity on you?' And in his

anger the master handed him over to the tortur-
ers till he should pay back all the debt. And this
is how my Father will deal with you unless you
each forgive your brother from your heart"
(Matthew 18:32–35).

Jesus was the brother who forgives. He for-
gave not only personal offenses, but also the
social offenses of public sinners, those offenses
which place a person outside of society—at
least outside of the society of "decent" folk. It
was not that he was in sympathy with such
people. By all his Judaic formation, Jesus must
have felt the same repugnance pious Jews felt
when they encountered persons catalogued as
sinners.

Such was the case of the publicans, the collectors of taxes. They worked at the service of
the Romans, which made them despicable to
the eyes of the faithful Jews. But Jesus went to
meet them in spite of the reputation of the
Pharisees: "It is not the healthy who need the
doctor, but the sick. I did not come to call the
virtuous, but sinners" (Mark 2:17). The parable
of the Pharisee and the publican illustrates this
conduct. The case of Zaccheus, who was a
high-ranking receiver of taxes, permitted Jesus

to affirm once again his unusual predilection. "The Son of Man has come to seek out and save what was lost" (Luke 19:10).

Women sinners were received in the same way. "I tell you that her sins, her many sins, must have been forgiven, or she would not have shown such great love. It is the man who is forgiven little who shows little love" (Luke 7:47). In the case of the woman surprised in adultery, Jesus said, "If there is one among you who has not sinned, let him be the first to cast a stone at her" (John 8:8).

## THE FOREIGNERS

This predilection of Jesus for sinners also made him accessible to foreigners. To the Jews, foreigners were pagans and were therefore sinners by their birth. It was pious and virtuous to stay away from them. The mission of Jesus did not take him outside the limits of the people of Israel (Matthew 15:25). He did not need to attend to the pagans who did not fall within his mission.

Despite this, he responded to the supplication of the Roman centurion: "Jesus showed amazement on hearing this and remarked to his followers, 'I tell you, nowhere in Israel have I found so much faith' " (Matthew 8:10). He also admired a Syro-Phoenician woman whose daughter was possessed by a devil. It was audacity on her part to risk coming near a Jew. Jesus told her: "The children should be fed first, because it is not fair to take the children's food and throw it to the house-dogs" (Mark 7:28). But the woman knew how to reply and Jesus helped her, even though he knew that in so doing he was aiding an enemy of his nation, a pagan, and therefore a public sinner.

In regard to the Samaritans who were quasi-pagans, Jesus chose one of them as the protagonist in his famous parable on charity toward one's neighbor. The image of the perfect brother was a Samaritan (Luke 10). While traveling through Samaria Jesus arrived at the well of Jacob. He treated the Samaritan woman who came to get water with such courtesy that the disciples were surprised (John 4:27).

## THE CHILDREN

Finally, those who received most of his attention were the little ones, the most rejected, those who were considered nothing. On a certain occasion, the disciples discussed who would be the greatest. Having seated himself, Jesus called the Twelve together and said to them: " 'If anyone wishes to be first, he must make himself last of all and servant of all.' Then he took a little child, stood him in their midst, and putting his arms around him, said to them, 'Anyone who welcomes one of these little children in my name, welcomes me' " (Mark 9:34–37). At that time the cult of the child did not exist. They were really the "little ones." People were bringing their little children to him to have him touch them, and the disciples were scolding them for this. Jesus became indignant when he noticed it and said to them: "Let the little children come to me; do not stop them; for it is to such as these that the kingdom of God belongs" (Mark 10:13–14). For him, the attraction of children lay in the fact that they did not have titles, nor dignity, nor were they regarded as important; very little notice was given them by their society.

To shelter and to serve what was looked down on and considered nothing in the eyes of men was what Jesus taught his disciples. He practiced it with extraordinary constancy. "You know that among the pagans, their so-called leaders lord it over them; and their great men make their authority felt. This is not to happen among you. No! Anyone who wants to be great among you must be your servant, and anyone who wants to be first among you must be slave to all. For the Son of Man himself did not come to be served but to serve and to give his life in ransom for many" (Mark 10:42–45).

If we attempt to understand the reason for this preference for the little ones, we need to interpret it within the total context of the mission of Jesus. If not, it can appear as a morbid deformation, an inclination to weakness, an incapacity to appreciate the values of life, and the deliberate seeking of refuge in pointless misery. We must look in just the opposite direction, if we want to understand this attitude of Jesus. His preference never directed itself toward weakness, sin, littleness for its own sake. It referred to a vision of the kingdom of God within the perspective of the people of Israel. Jesus came to save what was lost or considered lost. The Pharisees, the chiefs of the people, resigned themselves easily to the marginalizing of the poor or the non-integrated. Such people meant nothing to them. Jesus, however, believed in the vocation and value of all the people of Israel. He could not accept that anyone, no matter how insignificant he seemed, be lost or simply abandoned. If the Pharisees gladly sacrificed all those who did not follow their example, Jesus never resigned himself to this withdrawal. He went to seek the rejected, including those who had rejected themselves and thought themselves unworthy. This attitude of Jesus is exemplified in his parables of Luke 15: the lost sheep, the lost coin, the lost son. Jesus went to find "the lost sheep of the house of Israel" (Matthew 15:24). His passion was not for the misery of one rejected group; it was for all the people of Israel, for the idea of remaking the unity and lost brotherhood among human beings. The love of Jesus cannot be thought of as plain intimacy. Though existentialist theologians dwell on the intimate themes and preoccupation of the "I-thou" relationship, the love of Jesus was not of this kind. All his friendships, his preoccupations, his service, and his dedication integrated themselves in a total dedication of remaking the lost alliance of the people of God. This sign of Jesus' charity is perfectly expressed in the final prayer which John places in the discourse after the last supper: "That all may be one" (John 17:21).

To remake the brotherhood he had to begin with those who were furthest away—those fragments of Israel who were dispersed and had to be gathered together. The union could not be achieved by conquest or constraint. Those who had lost hope and who found themselves left out had to be recovered. This was the mission of Jesus. The Pharisees also wanted the unity of Israel. But they waited for God to achieve it miraculously; they did not want to go themselves, leaving the ninety-nine faithful sheep, to recover the last one who had lost his way. Their preoccupation with unity was only verbal. They did not act, because there was no love to stimulate and lead them.

Recovering the weak and the little ones demanded patience and indulgence. The Pharisees imposed the heavy weight of unreasonable precepts and works of insupportable piety. Jesus, on the other hand, said: "Come to me, all you who labor and are overburdened, and I will give you rest. Shoulder my yoke and learn from me, for I am gentle and humble of heart. And you will find rest for your souls. Yes, my yoke is easy and my burden light" (Matthew 11:28–30). The Pharisees limited the way of salvation by precepts and helped only those who fulfilled all the laws, thus driving the "lost" ones even further away.

However—and here is the paradox—the poor and the simple showed themselves more aware of their vocation, this vocation written in the Covenant of Israel from its beginnings, than those who considered themselves the pillars of the holy nation. What the parables contained in veiled form, they saw happening all around them: the parable of the murderous tenants (Matthew 21:33–43); the parable of the king who celebrated a wedding reception for his son (Matthew 22:1–14). At the response of some and the refusal to understand of others Jesus was able to give thanks to God: "I bless you, Father, Lord of heaven and of earth, for hiding these things from the learned and the clever, and revealing them to mere children" (Matthew 11:25).

Sometimes Jesus' love of the people of Israel and his preoccupation with their mission turned to indignation against those who used their privileges only for themselves, without accepting the vocation and the commitment that went with them. His indignation was also directed against the cities of Israel which had not responded to him while the poor and the miserable, including the sinners, understood. "Alas for you, Chorazin! Alas for you, Bethsaida! For if the miracles done in you had been done in Tyre and Sidon, they would have repented long ago, in sackcloth and ashes. And still I tell you that on judgment day it will not go as hard on Tyre and Sidon as with you. And as for you, Capernaum, did you want to be exalted as high as heaven? You shall be thrown down to hell. For if the miracles done in you had been done in Sodom, it would have been standing yet" (Matthew 11:20–23). "On judgment day, the men of Nineveh will stand up with the present generation and condemn it, because when Jonah preached, they repented; and there is something greater than Jonah here" (Matthew 12:41).

From indignation Jesus turned to lamentation over the capital of Israel, Jerusalem: "As he drew near and came in sight of the city, he shed tears over it and said, 'If you, in your turn, had only understood on this day the message of peace! But, alas, it is hidden from your eyes!'" (Luke 19:41–44). In the temple his lamentation turned to anger: "He went into the temple and began driving out those who were selling: 'According to Scripture,' he said, 'my house will be a house of prayer, but you have turned it into a robbers' den' " (Luke 19:45–46).

All these sentiments converged in a fundamental passion through which Jesus identified himself with the destiny of the people of Israel—that is, with that vocation of "universal brotherhood" in which the new alliance consisted. In view of this new alliance to which all were called, Jesus ignored all restrictions, all repugnancies. He went to meet sinners and the downtrodden; he looked for the very least and the abandoned; he let himself be monopolized by the sick and by the afflicted; he accepted pagans; and he condemned the rigidity and the pride of the "pious" of his nation.

## THE CHOSEN BROTHERS

There were some persons to whom Jesus felt himself a brother in a very special and personal way. They were the disciples whom he chose himself. It was to them Jesus referred after the resurrection in his meeting with the women: "Go and tell my brothers that they must leave for Galilee; they will see me there" (Matthew 28:10).

In reality, the gospels do not call too much

attention to the internal life of the group of disciples, nor to their relationship with Jesus. It is clear that his and their attention was not directed to themselves, but to the work they were to realize in common. Their common task united them. When Jesus called to Simon and Andrew, he said to them: "Follow me and I will make you fishers of men" (Mark 1:17). He did not say "I will make you my friends," though friendship was implicit in the mission.

The proper name of "friends" does not appear in the first gospels. In his later gospel, John explains the situation. According to him, the friendship of the disciples with Jesus was based on their association in a common task: "I call you friends, because I have made known to you everything I have learned from my Father" (John 15:15). Jesus did not call his followers to be friends, rather, he said, "I chose you, and I commissioned you to go forth and bear fruit" (John 15:16).

In truth, Jesus did not offer his disciples an easy destiny. The end reserved for them was the same one he accepted. "The pupil is not superior to his teacher, nor the slave his master" (Matthew 10:24). "Remember, I am sending you out like sheep among wolves; so be cunning as serpents, and yet as harmless as doves. Beware of men; they will hand you over to Sanhedrins" (Matthew 10:16–17).

Still, despite all the risks, the disciples accepted this unvoiced destiny, and did so with generosity: "We have put aside everything to follow you!" (Mark 10:28). Certainly, there was in this a sign of hopeful expectation and perhaps ambition, too. The disciples were mistaken about the length of time which separated them from the consummation of the kingdom of Christ. They lived in expectation of an imminent end. Because of this, their attitude has in it a kind of naiveté that is not an example for us. We know *today* that the end was *not* near, and consequently certain of their attitudes are inaccessible to us today. It is easier to say: "We have abandoned all," when this "all" must last only a few years. Sacrifice means little if one hopes to have all back within a short time. It is something else to accept sacrifice when one knows it is accepted for an entire lifetime, in the monotony of days which repeat themselves endlessly. The disciples were ambitious for thrones at the side of the throne of the great king (Mark 10:37). This ambition also has no meaning for us now. We are more modest now by force of circumstance.

Between Jesus and his disciples complete communication was impossible. Theirs was more the beginning of friendship rather than a mature one, an approximation rather than a communion. It could not be any other way. Jesus was the teacher who needed to teach; and all his gestures are the gestures of a teacher.

The gesture of washing the disciples' feet was made not so much as an attention to them as to teach them about the kind of life they would have to lead much later in community. "If I, then, the Lord and Master, have washed your feet, you should wash each other's feet. I have given you an example so that you may copy what I have done to you" (John 13:14–15).

Jesus' friendship with his disciples was always subordinated to his total plan, which included the mission of the whole Israel. Jesus saw everything in the perspective of what the prophets attributed to his people. His first love went to the whole of the people of Israel who were to be a sign and instrument of the redemption of all nations.

Incidentally, the synoptic gospels do not give

any consideration to the connection between this friendship between Jesus and his disciples and his commitment to the love of neighbor and the love of God. These syntheses appear only in the Gospel of John. They are a reflection of what occurred later on. The first gospels only show that the explicit preoccupations of Jesus were very practical. The teacher was preoccupied with the ordinary life of the disciples. Once the time came for them to prolong his mission, they, in their turn, had to show themselves like him with other people—with the poor, with sinners, with pagans, with the sick, with the little ones. This is what Jesus taught his community of followers to do. Because of this he made recommendations about the desire to be the greatest, the scandal of the little ones, the hunting of the lost sheep, fraternal correction, prayer in common, and the pardon of offenses (Matthew 18:1–35). Christian fraternal love grew out of a pedagogy of love for the redemption of Israel and of all nations.

## DEATH AND THE BROTHERS

If the death of Jesus was the price of his liberty, there was in it also great value of char-

ity and generosity. The bond between the
death of the servant of God and the salvation of
Israel and the nations is mysterious. Isaias 53
had already announced this mysterious bond.
The gospels do not clarify the question very
much. It is, however, the object of various
reflections in the epistles and John. It seems
probable that Jesus did not announce in very
explicit form the signification of his death. He
knew, however, that as the servant of God he
was called to "give his life in ransom for the
many" (Mark 10:45). This "many" was the
people of Israel with whom all other nations
would be finally associated. Jesus knew that the
love and the dedication he manifested during
the years of his mission, his passion for the
people of God and for the recovery of this
people, would take him even to corporal passion, total abandonment, and even death. Not
only would it be necessary to allow the sick, the
poor, and the sinner complete access to his time
and energies; this sacrifice would go on until
the end. Because of it, the death of Jesus was an
act of love. Later on, John would explain this
concept saying, "Jesus realized that the hour
had come for him to pass from this world to the
Father. He had loved those who were his in the

world, but now he showed how perfect his love was" (John 13:1). "A man can have no greater love than to lay down his life for his friends" (John 15:13).

If Jesus was eminently the "neighbor," the brother of all his brothers, he taught also that this love of neighbor was the true love of God. Love of God was the standard of the Jews, their reason to exist as a people, their title of glory in the midst of the nations. This was nothing new. And Jesus naturally agreed (Mark 12:29–30). The novelty of his teaching, however, consisted in putting next to this first precept a second one: "You must love your neighbor as yourself" (Mark 12:31). To make these two commandments one and to highlight it in such a way that in it would be contained the entire law was something intensly original. It was in the context of this law that Jesus composed and reconciled his two fundamental attitudes: his liberty and his fraternity. The singular quality of fraternal love is what makes people free of all laws, all evil, and slavery in every form. This service to his people and to the redemption of the lost sheep of Israel, taught by Jesus, constitutes the synthesis of liberty and fraternity. It is the perfect service to the brother as brother,

without frontier and without limit. It is liberation from all the powers which keep people in a
state of domination. In everything he did and
taught, Jesus looked for this new and definitive
alliance or covenant for his people; and to in-
sure it, he placed his life and death at their
service.

# CHAPTER IV

# *The Father*

## IN SPIRIT AND IN TRUTH

In our meditation on Jesus of Nazareth, we have not yet treated of the presence of God in his life. Why have we been so slow to come to it? The reason is that fundamentally the mission of Jesus can be examined in terms of two preoccupations or two principal focal points: the message of liberation, and the message of fraternity to remake the true and eternal covenant of Israel. In the gospel recollections, God stays very hidden. He occupies a very small place. To say this would have provoked amazement in readers in the past. Projecting onto the gospel their own intense religious and cultural preoccupations, Christians of other times did not perceive this disconcerting fact. It

went unnoticed that Jesus did not bind himself
to a set of religious practices and did not seem to
preoccupy himself with the religious practice of
his disciples. Not only did he avoid immersing
himself in the cult of his people, he never
founded any new cult of his own. There is in
the gospels, in this respect, a very significant·
silence. What was, then, the place that God
occupied in the life and mind of Jesus?

In the first place, we said he did not practice
the religious acts of his people. It seems he
emancipated himself and wanted to emancipate
the disciples. The evangelists never show us
Jesus exercising an act of cult. When he went to
the temple, he went to preach his word, or to
expel the sellers. He did not go to offer sacrifice, to participate in sacred ceremonies, or to
recite prayers. He used the temple as a tribunal
or a theater for his activities, in a totally sec-
ularized sense. The temple was the place where
many people met. For Jesus, the temple was
capable of being destroyed (Mark 13:2), because it did not fulfill any role in the true covenant. Soon "the hour is coming when you will
worship the Father neither on this mountain
nor in Jerusalem. . . . But the hour will
come—in fact, it is here already—when true

worshippers will worship the Father in spirit and truth; that is the kind of worshippers the Father wants" (John 4:21–23).

By this time, Jesus did not mean simply that his followers could build temples wherever they wanted. He meant that from then on the true worship of God would not essentially consist in constructing temples and exercising cult. Rather, it would consist of acting under the movement of the Spirit and the truth.

Jesus did not offer sacrifice, nor did he encourage his disciples to express conventional piety. He did not lead them in the temple liturgical rites. He did not visit the synagogue regularly. The gospel narratives show that when he went to the synagogue he did so to reveal himself, and not out of devotion. In this sense, neither Jesus nor the apostles were very religious.

When he attacked the Pharisees, Jesus wanted nothing of their "piety." "And when you pray, do not imitate the hypocrites; they love to say their prayers, standing up in the synagogues and at the street corners for people to see them" (Matthew 6:5). They "make a show of lengthy prayers" (Mark 12:40).

It is true that Jesus sometimes went to

Jerusalem to participate in the feasts. However, as we have said, we do not see him exercise any act of cult. When the group approached Jerusalem at the end of Jesus' ministry, during this last trip to the capital it was the apostles who asked: "Where do you want us to go, and make the preparations for you to eat the Passover?" (Mark 14:12). Jesus responded to their preoccupation. The feast of the Jews offered him the occasion of encountering the crowds. It did not awaken religious feelings in him.

More surprising yet is the fact that Jesus did not found a cult himself. He did not organize a new manner of adoring God, of giving him homage or presenting gifts and supplications to him. He did institute the Supper. But it is difficult to recognize in that Supper an act of worship. It was a communitarian sign whose significance is bound up with the institution of the new covenant, the newly founded pact of the new Israel. There was not in these circumstances any act of cult. Much later the Christians integrated the Eucharist into an act of worship. But this transformation was not made by Jesus, and there is no sign he even thought about it in this way. The Eucharist turned into the Mass within the context of Mediterranean civilization, as a cultural adaptation. The institution of the Supper itself was not essentially an act directed to God. There certainly did not appear any new liturgy.

Jesus prayed, but without ceremony. And when he prayed, Jesus isolated himself. He did not offer his disciples any model of how to conduct themselves in prayer. "In the morning, long before dawn, he got up and left the house and went off to a lonely place and prayed there" (Mark 1:35). On other occasions, Jesus left the crowd and "went off into the hills to pray" (Mark 6:46). What was it he did there? We have no idea. When the apostles were preoccupied about prayer, they appealed to the example of John the Baptist. They must have had the impression that Jesus himself was not interested in this subject. One of the disciples said to him: "Lord, teach us to pray just as John taught his disciples" (Luke 11:1). It is interesting that an explicit petition of the disciples, amazed at his conduct, was necessary before Jesus was moved to give the formula par excellence of Christian prayer.

In the matter of prayer, Jesus was discreet and wanted to maintain the privacy of the act. Not only did he himself neglect to speak of prayer with the disciples, but when he spoke, he spoke most often in the negative. "In your prayers do not babble as the pagans do, for they think that by using many words they will make themselves heard. Do not be like them" (Matthew 6:7–8). "But when you go to pray, go to your private room, and, when you have shut the door, pray to your Father who is in that secret place, and your Father who sees all that is done in secret will reward you" (Matthew 6:6). For Jesus the idea of prayer was accompanied by the idea of a hidden place. Discretion in the way to do it, in its quantity, and in its place. Everything happened as if Jesus wanted to make the exercise of prayer totally spontaneous and personal, without social conditions and without constraint. This prayer totally lacked display, ceremony, and external expression. It was not worship, but a familiar conversation.

The gospels do not describe any mystical manifestations in the life of Jesus. This indicates that the apostles were not present at any of his religious experiences, nor did Jesus think any profit would be gained in relating such experiences, if in fact he had them. In this manner, Jesus was very different from the Christian mystics who invoked him later.

Further, he never outlined any ascesis to facilitate the mystical life. The gospels do not show us a "religious" Jesus, but a person free of rites, ceremonies, formulas, and marked hours. This does not mean modern Christians cannot use such things. It simply means they are not able to invoke the example of Jesus to support them.

The unique religious phenomenon at which the gospels make us present is the Transfiguration. But even that was not really a religious phenomenon in the cultural sense. There was no cult, or formal homage. Jesus did not appear in a state of prayer or ecstasy. The disciples did not receive any instructions on how to treat God at that time, although Peter suggested building three shrines there to commemorate the event.

The prayers of Jesus which the gospels refer to were those of his passion. In the garden of the agony, Jesus prayed. "They came to a small estate called Gethsemane, and Jesus said to the disciples, 'Stay here while I pray.' Then he took Peter and James and John with him. And a sudden fear came over him, and great distress. And he said to them, 'My soul is sorrowful to the point of death. Wait here and keep awake.' And going on a little further, he threw himself on the ground, and prayed that, if it were possible, this hour might pass him by. 'Abba (Father)!' he said. 'Everything is possible for you. Take this cup away from me. But let it be as you, not I, would have it' " (Mark 14:32–36). In this prayer, there seems to have been no element of religious experience and no sensing of the presence of the Father. It was the prayer of the silence of God. No answer came. Much later, on the cross, Jesus pronounced his words of loneliness and abandonment: "My God, my God, why have you deserted me?" (Mark 15:34). There is no prayer more empty of any "mystical" experience. Still, the mystics will say no prayer is more truly mystical.

These negative observations are very significant for the "religion" instituted by Jesus. The Church later added an abundant liturgy. However, this liturgy did not exist in the beginning. It does not have the value of revelation that the life of Jesus has. In conclusion, the relationship of Jesus with the Father seems exceptionally free of any liturgical or cultural baggage. The unique cult which the Father seemed to desire of Jesus was his special mission, his journeys and voyages, the cures of the

sick, the instruction given to the crowds or to
the disciples or that which Paul would later call
"spiritual worship" (Romans 12:1).

## THE NAME OF GOD

Where, then, are the relations between Jesus
and God to be found? That is what we will look
for next.

First, what was the name Jesus himself used
to refer to God? Jesus did not propose any new
name. The divine name he used comes from the
Bible. Later the synoptic gospels practiced a
significant selection among all the divine
names. It cannot be doubted that the selection
had been made by Jesus and imitated by the
first Christians.

The gospel tradition did not avoid the name
of God (the Greek *theos* translates the Hebrew
name), as did the pious Jews of that time. It did
not practice, therefore, the pious religious re-
finements of the Pharisees. The only case
where the name of "God" is suppressed for
religious motives is in the use of the expression
"kingdom of heaven" in Matthew. It is, however, more probable that Jesus said "kingdom

of God," in accord with the tradition of Mark. The name "the most High" is used only occasionally in spite of being in common use among the Jews. The name of "King" only comes up once (Matthew 5:35), in a text that seems to refer to a citizen. In the same way the name "Lord" is encountered only in citations or in very solemn texts, despite its being habitually used among the Jews. Obviously these were not the names used by the first Christians. Jesus spoke another way.

The name of God most used by him was "Father." This name was not new. It already existed in the Old Testament, and it was well known in Jesus' time. Therefore, he did not invent it. It is only his insistence on this title that constitutes something new.

In Jesus' way of speaking, the name of "Father" becomes the proper name of God, so proper that it must be reserved to him alone. In Jesus' mind, that name was so uniquely God's that no one else could claim it. "You must call no one on earth your father, since you have only one Father, and he is in heaven" (Matthew 23:9). Besides this, the vocative "Father, Abba, Father!" used by Jesus is a new phenomenon.

The Jews did not address their God this way. There was, in Jesus' use of this expression, a tone of familiarity totally new. There was a total absence of ceremony. Because of this, it is not possible that so unrestrained an address was invented by the Christians. Only Jesus could have introduced this style.

The gospels knew various ways of using the title Father: "the Father," "my Father," "your Father." Certain texts are compositions of tradition, for example, the prayer of Jesus in the garden of Gethsemane. If the disciples were sleeping, they did not hear the prayer of Jesus. However, they could have placed in it the title "Father" only if they had preserved the memory of the habitual way that Jesus used it. Its inspiration and its creation were from Jesus.

God was Father to Jesus and also was Father to the disciples and humankind in general. There were two different relationships. The texts make clear that God was not Father in the same way in both cases. However, the fact that the same title could be attributed to him on the part of both shows there was contact between the two paternities. God's paternity of Jesus determined his paternity of people in general.

Also the filial attitude of people in general is derived from the attitude of Jesus.

## TO KNOW THE FATHER

Jesus spoke of the Father with much simplicity and familiarity. He permitted and suggested a similar attitude to his followers. Nonetheless, he did not give many explanations of God's nature. He did not give his disciples any doctrine about God, what he is like, what his attributes are, and so forth. The gospels do not expose the essence of God. In this they stand much behind the philosophers and the pagan religions. What was of interest to Jesus in his preaching was not speaking of God, but speaking of humankind and its future. The Father was always present, but always most discreetly. He remained hidden.

It is not by chance that the gospel traditions do not contain a revelation of God. The silence is deliberate. Jesus took on all the rigor of Hebrew theology in reverencing God: He left him where that theology put him—above his creatures in such a way that, although present everywhere, his privacy remains totally inviolable. "No one has ever seen God " (John 1:18).

Among the Jews it was considered idiocy, presumption, irreligiosity to try to know something of God.

Much later John would connect this inviolability of God with the fact of the life of Jesus. In that gospel, God remains inaccessible and inconceivable—after Jesus, as before. But he made himself known—or better still—gave a sign of his presence, in the occurrences of history. The significant happening, par excellence, was the passage of Jesus of Nazareth through the villages and roads of Palestine. Whoever sees and contemplates with attention this Jesus of Nazareth will understand all that can be understood of God in this world. "It is only the Son, who is nearest the Father's heart, who has made him known" (John 1:18). "Philip said: 'Lord, let us see the Father, and then we shall be satisfied.' 'Have I been with you all this time, Philip,' said Jesus to him, 'and you still do not know me? To have seen me is to have seen the Father, so how can you say, "Let us see the Father"? Do you not believe that I am in the Father and the Father in me?' " (John 14:8–10).

That is an answer which cannot mislead us. Jesus did not mean to say he had a God-like air. In him, divinity showed its presence under the form of human signs. There was nothing in his appearance which was not purely human. In Jesus, God did not cause himself to be visible; rather, through him, he showed the unique way which leads us securely to God. The message of Jesus consisted in affirming that there is nothing to be gained in wanting to know God himself, directly. The only way of knowing something about God now lay in knowing Jesus. He who entered on the way preached by his disciples learned to know their Master. In other words, accepting a prescribed way to be human and living as a human can constitute authentic access to God.

Therefore, if you wish to know God, you need to know how Jesus saw himself in relation to the Father. And if you wish to enter into the same relationship (in the measure which is possible), you must follow his example.

## SONSHIP

Jesus was extremely private about explaining his relation to the Father. Nevertheless it seemed clear he knew him well. He did not hesitate to speak in his name. He did not speak as the scribes, who made commentaries of the biblical texts, but as one who knew the Author of the Bible. At the same time, Jesus appeared totally submissive to the Father. It was not his own work he did; it was the work of the Father, for the service of his kingdom. All his effort was bent toward bringing about the kingdom. What set him apart was that he received this work directly from the Father, because he was sent by him.

John would later elaborate this relationship between the Father and the Son in explicit formulas. He said that Jesus was the Father's messenger sent to realize his works. The synoptic gospels remain much closer to the historic sources. They show Jesus doing this without expressing it in an explicit way.

Jesus was obedient to the Father according to the style and the form of the Jews. He read the Scriptures and discovered in them God's orders and instructions. As a servant of God, he submitted his mission and his entire activity to the word of the sacred book. The Bible is the written letter of God, to ambassadors sent to the people of Israel. In it, Jesus encountered the plan outlined by God. When he answered the temptations of Satan, he cited the biblical words by which the Israelites were called to fidelity and to submission (Matthew 4:4,7,10).

But the most interesting fact about Jesus' use of Scripture is that he claimed to interpret it correctly without referring to the scribes. He obeyed the spirit, not the letter, with the assurance of one who had access to the mind of the Writer. "Jesus had now finished what he wanted to say, and his teaching made a deep impression on the people, because he taught them with authority and not like their own scribes" (Matthew 7:28–29). Jesus' obedience to the Scripture was not simply submission to a written letter but submission to God. How did he know the mind of God, the true sense of the words? How did he arrive at the certainty that his interpretation, rather than the current one, might be true? He never gives us any psychological explanation.

The Pharisees invoked the tradition of the ancients to justify their way of understanding Scripture. Jesus denounced the hypocrisy of their projecting their own mentality into the text, choosing what suited them, distorting the true context of the precepts: "Why do you, for your part, act contrary to the commandment of God for the sake of your 'tradition' ?" (Matthew 15:3).

But it was not only the scribes and the Pharisees that Jesus contradicted. He went even to the point of contradicting Moses himself; he made himself a judge of Moses. For example, he spoke of the weakness in Moses' teaching on divorce. He invoked Genesis 2:24 against the law of Moses: "So then, what God has united, man must not divide" (Matthew 19:6). How to explain the contradiction of Moses? "It was because you were so unteachable, that Moses allowed you to divorce your wives," he replied, "but it was not like this from the beginning. Now I say this to you: The man who divorces his wife," etc. (Matthew 19:8-9). In the Sermon on the Mount, the first gospel brings together other sentences in which Jesus rectifies, in a similar way, the precepts of Moses (Matthew 5:21,27,31,33,38,43).

The obedience of Jesus to his Father was directly inspired by the mission God had given him. It was beyond the letter of the Scriptures. It was not out of insubordination, therefore, but from greater subordination, that he corrected or interpreted the texts.

Some specialists think the citations placed by the evangelists in the mouth of Jesus are the work either of oral tradition or of the editors.

Nevertheless, there can be no doubt that the editors or the tradition itself remembered very clearly the very way Jesus acted. They knew the Master cited the biblical words, though naturally they would not be able to guarantee that Jesus cited exactly such and such a word in every discourse.

Fundamentally, to be Son of the Father meant having received from him a mission, and subordinating one's whole life to this mission. It meant placing all moments of existence, all decisions, all options under the direction of his Word. On the other hand, Jesus himself acted as though he believed that the Father did not determine the content of his concrete acts. In the Scriptures God had traced the fundamental lines of the existence of Jesus, but God did not intervene and dictate the applications in the details of that existence. He left the task of incarnating the outlines of the plan in concrete circumstances entirely to his Son. The Father defined the ideal, without describing it in the real context of a life. It was for Jesus to discover the concrete way which would most faithfully translate the ideal. The obedience of Jesus was not passive, as it would be were he simply executing a completed plan with fidelity. It was

instead an active obedience which created a
human existence never before lived in the concrete, on the basis of certain fundamental inspi-
rations. For the people of his time, it was
enough to re-read the texts of the Old Testament invoked by Jesus to justify his way of life,
and to verify that, in fact, the instructions of the
Father remained sufficiently undetermined as
to allow him such freedom of action. Until
Jesus, no Jew had understood the true depth of
the Word of God. Jesus, however, penetrated
this word to its deepest sense, and created a
valid concrete realization of it in his life.

## GRASP OF LIFE EXPERIENCE

Though the gospels do not provide us any
abstract doctrine about the Father, if we start
with the life of Jesus, we can construct the
pattern of how we too must live if we would be
his children. We know the Father through a
way of life. Jesus showed us that the important
thing is not to invoke constantly the name of
God, but to live in a way which corresponds to
the Father's will. The Father does not want his
children to stay always preoccupied with him;
he wants them to realize his plan for the world

and fulfill the mission he gives them. "It is not those who say to me, 'Lord, Lord' who will enter the kingdom of heaven, but the person who does the will of my Father in heaven" (Matthew 7:21). "What is your opinion? A man had two sons. He went and said to the first, 'My boy, you go and work in the vineyard today.' He answered, 'I will not go,' but afterwards thought better of it and went. The man then went and said the same to the second, who answered, 'Certainly sir,' but did not go. Which of the two did the Father's will? 'The first,' they said" (Matt. 21:28–31). We conclude the important thing is not to say, but to do.

In this, Christianity is different from all the known religions. Jesus revealed an unknown God: a God who is not interested in cult, but in a human existence dedicated to the service of humanity. Jesus came "not to be served but to serve, and to give his own life as a ransom for many" (Matthew 20:28). The Father needs no homage or acclaim. His one desire is that his mission of serving humanity be fulfilled.

Under these conditions, dedication to a cult cannot be thought of as the true service of God. God does not need slaves. The service of God takes the form of a mission to be accomplished.

Obedience to God is realized in the application of all human energies to creating constantly a life which fulfills the mission received. Jesus obeyed the Father, not in the temple of Jerusalem offering sacrifice, but on the roads of Galilee realizing his mission of preacher, miracle worker, and witness.

This relation of creative obedience was reflected in the relationship of Jesus with the material world and with humankind.

In the first place, we see repercussions of the service of the Father towards the material world. We have considered how Jesus, by the radical acceptance of his mission, made himself free and untroubled about his situation in the exterior world. He was free of fear and anxiety. In the ultimate stronghold of his personality, he was invulnerable. Even in the worst moments of his existence, acceptance of his mission was more profoundly rooted there than was anxiety. Fear did not succeed in disturbing those roots by which Jesus was attached to his mission. Hence those famous texts: "I am telling you not to worry about your life. . . . Your heavenly Father feeds them. . . . So do not worry. . . . Your heavenly Father knows you need them all. . . . So do not worry about tomorrow. Tomorrow will take care of itself. Each day has enough trouble of its own" (Matthew 6:25–34).

The only way to live in the face of the world and stay truly free is to have confidence in the Father. But this confidence cannot be just in sentiment or verbal declaration. Jesus did not merely feel this confidence as a religious or mystical experience. He lived it, sustained by submission to his proper mission as the living condition of fidelity. Jesus' prayer, the "Our Father," expresses a victory over preoccupation and anxiety: "Give us today our daily bread" (Matthew 6:11). The attitude of abandonment shows itself again, for example, by confidence in prayer: "Ask and it will be given to you; search and you will find; knock and the door will be opened to you. For the one who asks, always receives; who searches always finds; the one who knocks will always have the door open to him. Is there a man among you who would hand his son a stone when he asks for bread, or would hand him a snake when he asks for a fish? If you, then, who are evil, know how to give your children what is good, how much more will your Father in Heaven give good things to those who ask him!" (Matthew 7:7–11).

This was an audacious counsel for Jesus to give, because he knew very well that the Father will not necessarily satisfy all the desires of his children in the form that they desire it. God will not really give his children all they ask for. He will give better things.

Detachment, such as Jesus taught, frees people from the pressures exercised on them by worry about money. In this respect Jesus was completely free. Dedicated to his mission, he received and took advantage of the resources offered to him. As to the future, he confided in the Father, which meant he asked no guarantee, renounced his own desires, and disposed himself to being content with what would come.

In effect, obedience to the Father is incompatible with love of money: "You cannot be the slave both of God and money" (Matthew 6:24). Service of the Father liberates, and service of money enslaves. From this comes the affinity between the poor and the Father, a constant theme of the gospels. Jesus knew quite well that money confers power, fame, and esteem in the midst of people and that poverty separates people. The parable Jesus told his disciples about the temptations of Satan shows he understood the lure of money. But at the same time, he knew that no one is able to gain money—and with it the world—without adoring Satan. Here is the dilemma between the two sole options: "I will give you all these," Satan said, "if you fall at my feet and worship me." And Jesus replied, "You must worship the Lord your God, and serve him alone" (Matthew 4:10). That is, either seek after money and use the means for this end, which, in concrete, constitutes the cult of Satan, or renounce money and accept poverty, which makes service—the true cult of God—possible.

In the face of political power, as well, service of the Father makes people free: "Give back to Caesar what belongs to Caesar, and to God what belongs to God" (Mark 12:17). Whatever the interpretation of this enigmatic counsel, one thing is certain: Here Jesus again takes an attitude of independence, and clearly distinguishes between the service of Caesar and the service of God. Without degrading the first, he refuses to let it influence the second. During the passion, the behavior of Jesus before the representative of Caesar corresponded to this declaration.

Furthermore, the relation between Jesus and

the Father freed him from social competition. He never had to defend himself on that ground. Because out of love for his Father he refrained from competition for material goods and was disposed to sacrifice everything—even life itself—for his mission, he won the love of the people. From the beginning, loving God was the first precept of the law of Moses (Deuteronomy 6:4–5). The Pharisees, however, had reduced the love of God to the rigid observance of a catalog of material precepts. They said they loved God, but in reality they did not even know what real love was. "Alas for you, Pharisees! because you . . . disregard justice and the love of God" (Luke 11:42). The Pharisees were disconcerted with this accusation, since they thought themselves totally dedicated to the love of God. They had thoroughly misled themselves about the meaning of this love.

True love of God lives in the love of people, in imitation of the love of the Father for people. This is what the Pharisees did not know, and what Jesus revealed. In this consists all perfection: "You must therefore be perfect just as your heavenly Father is perfect" (Matthew 5:48). "Love your enemies and pray for those who persecute you. In this way, you will be sons of your Father in Heaven, for he causes his sun to rise on bad men as well as good, and his rain to fall on honest and dishonest men alike" (Matthew 5:44–45). Jesus was a true son of the Father, eminently so, because his whole life was an illustration of his love of God. We never see him explain a dialogue between the Father and himself. The only words the gospels place in his mouth as being directed to the Father are monologues. The Father never answers. There is no I-Thou feeling to it. The real dialogue between Jesus and the Father was a concretely lived life of total service to humankind.

Such are the signs of the Father which Jesus left us. We must recognize—even if they disturb some of our comfortable old religious notions—their undeniable originality. This does not dispute the value of cult or the value of religious experience as the Church accepts or organizes them. But meditation on and imitation of the life of Jesus provide the sole norms by which his would-be followers must judge themselves.

# CHAPTER V

# *The Hope*

## NEW COVENANT

We have already spoken many times of Jesus' mission, and we have said that everything he did was related to the consciousness he had of that mission. Such being the case, we should now give closer attention to this mission. Outside the context of a total vision of time and of the future that the Gospels await and frequently explain, however, an understanding of it is impossible. Jesus saw his personal mission within the perspective of the evolution of united humanity. He learned from Judaism that the history of every person takes its value from the design of God as it relates to the entire nation. Jesus did not present himself as a great philosopher or a wise man or a personality whose individual action would have influence on people. He knew himself to be an instrument of the history which surrounded him and gave him his significance. He interpreted his role within the context of his people's hope. In the very center of his being was a great hope—a hope which coincided with the hope of Israel. It is appropriate, therefore, to meditate first on the hope of Jesus.

The most ancient documents of the traditions about the facts and the sayings of Jesus contain few references to the hope of Israel. There was no need to state again what was still evident. For the first Christians, it was much too clear that all the acts of Jesus presupposed the history and the messianic hopes of Israel. The gospels which were written especially for the Greeks (those of Luke and John) are the ones most careful to explain this hope which was the key to all his words and acts.

In a certain way, in the famous canticle of Zechariah, Luke presented a synthesis of the hope of Israel. He wanted to record for the least initiated readers the environment in which the message of Jesus sounded: The messenger of God is come, it said, he is alive: He who would "save us from our enemies and from the hands of all who hate us. Thus he shows mercy to our ancestors, thus he remembers his holy covenant, the oath he swore to our father Abraham that he would grant us; free from fear, to be delivered from the hands of our enemies, to serve him in holiness and virtue in his presence all our days" (Luke 1:71–75).

There was in Israel—and this hope was maintained constantly, at least among the poor—a confidence that the prophecies would be realized. There was the conviction that what was said in the past and written in the sacred books concerning the purpose of Israel was an announcement and a prophecy of the future. All that which had been expressed in the past was only a figure and a preparation for a future destiny. "The glory of Israel" would be revealed in the future. The Israelites hoped for this "glory of your people Israel" (Luke 2:32).

Over the years, the prophets had remembered this "glory of Israel"; and Jesus knew his mission was situated in this hope. In the end, in the day marked by God, in the awaited time, Israel would finally be the people of God, free and fraternal—the people in which all would be kings and priests, in which all would reveal the word of God, in which "peace" would overflow (Luke 1:79; 2:14), the fulness and the harmony of all blessings.

We cannot begin to understand the mission of Jesus unless we start from this one fact: Jesus assumed in his person the totality of his people's exceptional hope. He was, in fact, an amplifier of this hope. He did not bother much about the present, but looked constantly beyond the visible present. He was a man who lived in harmony with realities which were to come, but which had not yet appeared.

Jesus was not, primarily, the proof of the God who lives in the heavens. He was not the manifestation of an immutable knowledge of an immutable God. He was, above all, the announcer of a God who comes. He lived intensely this awareness of the coming of God on earth in the midst of people. And the first to be affected by this coming were the Jews.

One who is not Jewish cannot possibly imagine the importance of this hope. Christians, born as gentiles, cannot understand the intensity with which Jesus lived the prophecies that referred to the destiny of Israel. Not only did he try to give new life to the old prophecies; he knew, that from then on, the time of their realization was imminent. He felt he had arrived at the time in which the entire past of Israel would assume its significance. The hour, awaited for so many centuries, had struck. The time to be alert and attentive had arrived. Because of this, it was urgent to awaken all of Israel to its destiny.

Thus we have the mission given to the disciples: "Do not turn your steps to pagan territory and do not enter any Samaritan town; go rather after the lost sheep of the House of Israel" (Matthew 10:6). "I tell you solemnly, you will not have gone the rounds of the towns of Israel before the Son of Man comes" (Matthew 10:23).

Besides miracles, signs of mercy, pardon of sins, cures of the sick, and announcement of the gospel to the poor, all the activity of Jesus related to the prophecies. Much later the gospels insisted on recalling the best-known texts of this prophetic vision.

The special calling of the disciples involved the destiny of Israel: "You will yourselves sit on twelve thrones to judge the twelve tribes of Israel" (Matthew 19:28). The passion of Jesus was the new passover, the definitive passage of Israel to the new land. Finally, the ultimate sign, that of the Supper, powerfully evoked the covenant of Israel. It was the definitive renewal of this alliance. Jesus placed his earthly work and his death under the sign of the covenant: He fulfilled the acts which, it was foretold, would complete the covenant "for the forgiveness of sins" (Matthew 26:28).

The promises made to the poor and the humble include all the blessings which result from this agreement and are encountered in the fulfillment of this passover: "Happy" . . . because "theirs is the kingdom of heaven," . . . because "they shall be comforted," . . . because "they shall have the earth for their heritage," . . . because "they shall be satisfied," . . . because "they shall see God," . . . because "they shall be called sons of God" (Matthew 5:3–10). All these formulas are the equivalents of the covenant blessings. All record the message of the prophets. All show that the promises of Jesus were for people to transmit and cultivate. And with his coming, they spoke at last of a future soon to come.

## LIGHT OF NATIONS

Jesus knew hardly any place outside Israel. He did not work among the pagans. His perspective was always circumscribed by Israel. Nevertheless, within the mission of Israel fell, in accord with the prophets, the salvation of all nations. It was in the idea of the prolongation of the destiny of Israel that Jesus saw the other nations of the earth. It was through the mediation of the mission and the destiny of Israel that he reached out to them. He knew that it was Israel's vocation to illuminate all nations. This is an aspect of the hope of the prophets he particularly accentuated.

In another passage, Luke points out the universality of the prophetic promises. The canticle of Zechariah celebrated "the tender mercy of our God, who, from on high, will bring the Rising Sun to visit us, to give light to those who live in darkness and the shadow of death" (Luke 1:78–79).

This salvation of Israel, which was for others as well, was mentioned by the ancient Simeon: "Because my eyes have seen the salvation which you have prepared for all nations to see, a light to enlighten the pagans and the glory of your people Israel" (Luke 2:30–32).

It is in this perspective we must see the value of all that Jesus did, as precursory signs of this illumination for all nations: in the answer given to the Roman centurion and to the Syro-

Phoenician woman, in the cursing of the cities of Israel, and in the comparison with the pagan cities, who received with more attention the warnings of the prophets.

It is not strange that after the resurrection the mission of the disciples to the foreign nations started. This mission was already announced in a certain way in the acts and words of Jesus. "Go out to the whole world; proclaim the Good News to all creation" (Mark 16:15).

## DENIAL BY ISRAEL

In point of fact, though, Jesus' hope met with a terrible obstacle. How could he believe in the mission of his people and reconcile this mission with his conviction of being its privileged instrument, when the people themselves withdrew from him? Unhappily, such was his experience. Not only did those groups most representative of the people of Israel refuse to accept him, they set themselves in radical opposition to him. The scribes, elders, priests, Sadduccees, and Herodians all separated themselves from him. The only understanding that he met with came from the ignorant poor of Galilee. He presented himself as the answer to the hope of his people, only to be rejected by them.

How then, was he able to persevere in the face of such a contradiction of facts? Not to lose heart, not to want to disappear back into Nazareth to take up the work of a carpenter again, he needed an incredible amount of conviction. And he had it. Nothing seemed able to take from him the soul and the will to go on.

Even more, the denial made by the representative leaders of Israel seems actually to have spurred Jesus on to threats and promises of judgment. The resistance of the leaders, he believed, could not win against the plan of God; those who opposed that plan would be judged and destroyed by the judgment of God.

Jesus encountered very strong arguments for his position in Israel's own history. Had not opposition to the messenger of God appeared again and again through sacred history whenever the prophets came? Jesus interpreted the hostility of the Jews to him in the light of the persecution of the prophets. And they, when they encountered opposition, far from losing heart, had answered it with judgment. Was not then this new resistance to God a sign that the judgment was near?

Serpents, brood of vipers! How can you escape condemnation to hell? This is why in my turn I am sending you prophets and wise men and scribes: Some you will slaughter and crucify, some you will flog in your synagogues and hunt down from town to town; and so you will draw down on yourselves the blood of every holy man that has been shed on earth from the blood of Abel the Holy to the blood of Zechariah, son of Barachiah whom you murdered between the sanctuary and the altar. I tell you solemnly, all of this will recoil on this generation (Matthew 23:33–36).

Jerusalem, Jerusalem, you that kill the prophets and stone those who are sent to you! (Matthew 23:37).

It is clear that Jesus was profoundly disturbed, emotional, and agitated by his persecution. He did not want to delude himself about it; he confronted it. The gospels give us three announcements of his final persecutions unto death, proof that this forthcoming tragedy had been called to the attention of the disciples, even though they remained inclined to false hopes. But the prophetic temperament of Jesus reacted emotionally, provoking his violent announcement of the judgment of God and the destruction of Israel. "Jesus left the temple and, as he was going away, his disciples came up to draw his attention to the temple buildings.

He said to them in reply: 'You see all these? I tell you solemnly, not a single stone here will be left on another: Everything will be destroyed' " (Matt. 24:1–2). "Then there will be great distress such as, until now, since the world began, there never has been nor ever will be again. . . . Immediately after the stress of those days, the sun will be darkened, the moon will lose its brightness, the stars will fall from the sky, and the powers of heaven will be shaken" (Matt. 24:29–30). These predictions were not original. They could be found in the books of the prophets. Jesus called attention to them in response to his foresight of future persecution. Far from being a sign of the hostility of God, far from being an attempt to stop a desperate undertaking, persecution, Jesus knew, must animate and strengthen the true servant of God. The certainty of the coming judgment was the thing which gave him hope in the midst of persecution. This persecution appeared so inevitable to the eyes of Jesus that he foresaw it not only for himself, but also for his disciples: "They will hand you over to be tortured and put to death; and you will be hated by all nations on account of my name. And then many will fall away; men will betray one another and

hate one another" (Matthew 24:9–10). Then
would appear the Son of Man sent by God to
realize the judgment. Then would appear the
truth, and those who had condemned Jesus
would be beaten and shamed. "Then the sign of
the Son of Man will appear in heaven; then too,
all the peoples of the earth will beat their
breasts; and they will see the Son of Man coming on the clouds of heaven with power and
great glory" (Matthew 24:30).

It was thus that the hope of Jesus overcame
the opposition of the nation. In spite of the
resistance of facts, he did not cease to believe
the opposition of Israel was further corrobora-
tion of the words of the prophets in respect to
the final judgment of God.

## REMNANT OF ISRAEL

Notwithstanding, one problem remained,
even if the judgment proved Jesus correct: How
was he to reconcile this final victory with the
hope that he was to be the redeemer and the
unifier of Israel? To the reader today this problem does not seem fundamental. For a Jew of
the first century and for Jesus, who thought of

using every moment of his life working for the destiny of Israel, the problem was fundamental indeed.

Jesus reconciled the apparently unreconcilable elements of his vision of the world and of his hope by giving to his disciples the vocation and mission of Israel. In the Scriptures there were a sufficient number of texts that, properly understood, showed that the true people of God were the poor and humble of Israel, the persecuted and humiliated. Therefore Jesus' disciples would be just that: the true Israel of fishermen and publicans, simple, unlearned people. They would be able to reconstitute the people of God and to illuminate the nations. On the day of judgment it was they who would occupy the thrones of the attendants of the Son of Man, in the place of the scribes, the ancients, and the priests. They would be the Sanhedrin of the true Israel after they had fulfilled the mission of realizing the prophecies.

Thus there was no reason to abandon the hope of Israel. Jesus never thought that he himself would be able to realize the whole assignment. From the beginning he knew that only one part of the destiny of Israel fell on him.

Because of this he chose his disciples and made them his continuers. In a special way, the mission of taking the light to the pagan nations would be reserved to the apostles. And this mission would be fulfilled before the day of the final judgment: "This Good News of the kingdom will be proclaimed to the whole world as a witness to all the nations. And then the end will come" (Matthew 24:14).

## KINGDOM OF GOD

In the midst of all these happenings, and because of them, Jesus saw the coming of that inevitable reality: the kingdom of God. This concept of the kingdom of God was his creation, one of the few concepts which were really his. We already know that the majority of his concepts came from the Old Testament, that is, from the people of whom it spoke. Since the concept of the kingdom of God was Jesus' creation, we are free to think he gave it a great deal of importance. We know that this concept did not exist among the people of Israel, that it was so original that not even the apostles were faithful to it. They cited it in the gospels and they attributed it to Jesus, only because Jesus used it. They did not use it, simply because they themselves did not know precisely what he meant. It did not serve them in expressing their experience of Christ.

But in the mind of Jesus, the kingdom of God united all the aspects of his presence, synthesizing not only the goal but also the provocations and resistances. The kingdom of God signified that God would reign, that God would triumph over his enemies and would establish his rule. It signified that a new people would begin and that the kingdom of God would be this new people in whom God reigns. This kingdom of God would be the restoration of the true Israel, the illumination of the nations, the judgment of the persecutors (the false Israel which kills the prophets), and the reunion of the elect from the four corners of the earth, as well as all the happenings which lead to these realities. We can believe that Jesus perceived all the aspects of the kingdom only bit by bit. From the beginning he had separated himself from the traditional objects of the hopes of Israel to choose this original concept. He knew from the start that it was his mission to give reality to the hope by collecting into a final synthesis the elements which were already in the Scriptures.

From beginning to end, Jesus was the witness of the announcement of the kingdom, and he lived so as to give evidence to his hope: "The time has come," he said, "and the kingdom of God is close at hand. Repent and believe the Good News" (Mark 1:15). He wanted the disciples to remain totally dedicated to it: "Set your hearts on his kingdom first, and on his righteousness, and all these other things will be given to you as well" (Matthew 6:33). His prayer would be "your kingdom come" (Matthew 6:10).

The signs and the words of Jesus confirmed the closeness of the kingdom. The opposition they encountered, the disciples just as much as Jesus, was a proof of its reality. This was really the mystery of the kingdom. Mystery here means "secret." The kingdom of God at first seems very modest. It grows starting from a very small seed (Matthew 13:31). It is so tiny that it seems hidden as yeast is in dough (Matthew 13:33). It comes and grows in the midst of people as a seed that matures alone: "This is what the kingdom of God is like. A man threw seed on the land. Night and day, while he sleeps, when he is awake, the seed is sprouting and growing; how, he does not know" (Mark 4:26–27).

The kingdom of God must endure opposition and persecution because God tolerates the presence of cockle in the field of wheat and the presence of the bad fish along with good fish in the net. So too, the word of the kingdom falls little by little on different soils, receives very different cultivations. The kingdom of God grows simultaneously with the mission of Jesus and the disciples. This hope cannot be destroyed, and it is not in vain that the disciples must leave all to buy the hidden treasure or the pearl of great price. To them "the mysteries of the kingdom of heaven are revealed" (Matthew 13:11).

Also, Peter receives the promise of the "keys of the kingdom of heaven" (Matthew 16:19) to give continuity to the mission of Jesus in the midst of this nucleus of the true Israel which consists of the reunion of the people of God.

Even with this, Jesus taught that the kingdom would know its decisive phase only in the day of the great judgment, when the Son of Man made the separation between the elect and the false members of the people of Israel: "The Son of Man will send his angels and they will gather out of his kingdom all things that provoke offenses, and all who do evil. . . . Then the virtuous will shine like the sun in the kingdom of their Father" (Matthew 19:41–43). "And I tell you that many will come from the east and the west and will take their places with Abraham and Isaac and Jacob at the feast in the kingdom of heaven; but the subjects of the kingdom will be turned out into the dark, where there will be weeping and grinding of teeth" (Matthew 8:11–13).

## WHEN?

It is certain Jesus could not have had the vision of history we have. He was not able to foresee the twenty centuries that separated us from him. When the disciples asked him a question in regard to the destruction of the temple of Jerusalem—"Tell us, when is this going to happen, and what sign will there be?"—Jesus answered, "As for that day or hour, nobody knows it, neither the angels of heaven nor the Son; no one but the Father" (Mark 13:31–32).

This ignorance of Jesus referred to the time of the events: namely, those events which affected Jerusalem, the temple, the people of Israel, the mission to the nations, the arrival of the Son of Man, and the diverse signs announced as forerunners.

But everything indicated that Jesus foresaw a rapid denouement. He did not imagine a long time of waiting. The texts the evangelists preserved for us create the impression that Jesus expected a very proximate end. Such texts did not aid the redactors in understanding the gospels, nor would they be easily understood by the first Christians. It is quite impossible that they could have been invented. It is precisely because they are difficult to understand and to accept that we can be sure that the words are of Jesus himself.

They include, for example, the following: "I tell you solemnly, before this generation has passed away all these things will have taken place" (Mark 13:30). "If they persecute you in one town, take refuge in the next. . . . I tell you solemnly you will not have gone the rounds of the towns of Israel before the Son of Man comes" (Matthew 10:23). "I tell you solemnly, there are some standing here who will not taste death till they see the kingdom of God come with power" (Mark 9:1).

These declarations, pronounced with such great gravity, are very obscure. In any case, a delay of many centuries stretching into the future cannot be reconciled with them. Probably, then, Jesus found himself in the same psychological dilemma that we have so often seen among the prophets of the Old Testament. The prophets never received revelations about time and the length of time. They saw the future with such clarity and certainty that the force of the vision made it seem imminent. They tended to reduce the length of time that separated them from the happenings. After the prophecies, history shows that these events took more time to happen than was foreseen. Furthermore, the prophets often placed successive happenings in a single simultaneous perspective. The same thing happened in the case of Jesus. The very force of his hope led him to see as immediate things that would take a long time. This same hope led him to see in one picture events which would be successive, which would happen at very great intervals. Jesus saw in one vision his death, the mission of the apostles, the end of the temple of Jerusalem, and the coming of the Son of Man—as if all this were to happen in the passing of one generation. He himself said the Father left him in ignorance—in other words that, concretely, he left him guided only by the outlines and the ways of thinking which were current among the people of Israel. In these conditions, it was inevitable that Jesus thought in the categories of the prophets and his contemporaries. For him, the time of the church would only be the length of one generation.

Much later, little by little, the disciples had to re-examine the prophecies of Jesus because of the passage of time and to deepen what he had said to them to meet the situation in which they found themselves.

To us today it appears incredible that Jesus remained so ignorant of the future of the church and that he did not think of planning the mission of the disciples. In fact, he did not leave any instructions at all except the mission to preach through the entire world. As to the internal life of the group and to the development of what would be the Christian church, he left only some recommendations of humility and charity. He assembled the Twelve and left them the continuation of his work. To Peter he gave a special mission. He recommended that the Supper be celebrated in his memory and as a sign of the new covenant sealed on the cross. Nothing more. This means he left his own work at the end of a rapid career with an immense confidence in the providence of God. He left everything to the Father. The future did not preoccupy him, and he did not worry about the future action of the disciples. He lived his own recommendation: Sufficient unto the day are its own evils.

This confidence in the Father showed the measure of his hope: "One man sows; another reaps" (John 4:37). He planted. He was certain others would go on to gather. What was to happen in the meantime would be achieved by the Father. It was not his problem. The Spirit would accompany the apostles and inspire them as to how to prolong his action until the end.

The last recommendations he left to his followers were recommendations of vigilance: They should always be alert, always ready and attentive to the signs of the kingdom of God. It is clear this recommendation takes for us, today, other nuances. In actual history, the

Father showed that the coming about of the kingdom would be much slower, complex, mysterious, and progressive  than Jesus in his human mind was to conceive it. Just the same, Jesus' recommendation is always valuable.

"Be on your guard, stay awake, because you never know when the time will come. It is like a man traveling abroad. He has gone from home and left his servants in charge, each with his own task; and he has told the doorkeeper to stay awake. So stay awake, because you do not know when the master of the house is coming: evening, midnight, cock-crow, or dawn; if he comes unexpectedly, he must not find you asleep. And what I say to you, I say to all: Stay awake" (Mark 13:33–37). The Gospel of Matthew added to these warnings a series of parables (Matthew 24:32–35,13). The conclusion is always the same: "So stay awake because you do not know the day or the hour" (Matthew 25:13).

The Pharisees did not understand the signs Jesus gave. "But you cannot read the signs of the times. It is an evil and unfaithful generation that asks for a sign. The only sign it will be given is the sign of Jonah" (Matthew 16:34). The Pharisees could not understand because they had already closed their minds. They decided on the criteria which would permit them to foresee the movement of God's will. They thought they understood all. Actually because of this, they understood nothing. Remain watchful, Jesus said. Watch out for the signs of the times, and foremost among them the sign of Jonah. He recommended also that the disciples remain listening and watchful because the kingdom of God was still coming. Even now, his work is not yet finished.

# CHAPTER VI

# *The Mission*

## PROPHET

In just what way did Jesus understand his work? Essentially as a mission, and this mission has to be interpreted within the vision of history that he himself conceived and presented to the disciples. Jesus understood that his life had already been written in the sacred book. Therefore, everything had to be performed in accord with the Scriptures. His life did not belong to him. In this, he could compare himself to the prophets of his nation, for the prophets also did not belong to themselves, but to God who chose them.

We must begin our meditation upon the mission of Jesus by seeing him as a prophet. In the life of Israel, the prophet was a profoundly representative figure, and the mission of Jesus was entirely bound up with the destiny of Israel. Of all the historical roles lived in the past, the one closest to the mission of Jesus was that of the prophet: neither priest, nor king, nor scribe, nor wise man offers so close a comparison, nor did Jesus think of himself in those categories. Jesus compared himself with the prophets and accepted the parallel.

The prophet is the man that God chose to realize his plans in Israel, and to be the carrier of his words and his signs. Jesus was the man of Israel until the end. He was bound to the destiny of Israel. He was this to such a point that it seems strange to us. While the church born of him has spread throughout the entire world, ostensibly showing a universal character, Jesus himself remained attached to the people of Israel, the old Israel of Moses and the prophets. He announced the preaching of his message to the pagans, but he himself did not go out to seek them. He accepted them when they presented themselves with great persistence, but he did not try to bring them to himself. "I was sent only to the lost sheep of the House of Israel" (Matthew 15:24). He knew that his mission was partial. He would not do everything. Others would do the rest. He stayed within the frontiers of his people. In this sense, Jesus announced the church, but did not found it in the time of his mortal life.

Jesus appeared as a Jewish prophet. Those who saw him thought of him that way. "And meanwhile, King Herod had heard about him, since by now his name was well known. Some were saying, 'John the Baptist has risen from the dead, and that is why miraculous powers are at work in him.' Others said, 'He is Elijah'; others again, 'He is a prophet like the prophets we used to have.' But when Herod heard this he said, 'It is John whose head I cut off; he has risen from the dead!' " (Mark 6:14–16). Herod was superstitious, but the others were right. When Jesus asked his disciples, "Who do people say that I am?" (Mark 8:27), he received a similar answer: " 'John the Baptist' they said. Others, 'Elijah,' others again, 'One of the prophets' " (Mark 8:28).

Jesus was not Elijah. "However, I tell you, Elijah has come" (Mark 9:13). Thus he compared himself with Elijah and his destiny with that of Elijah. He appealed to Elijah: "I tell you solemnly, no prophet is ever accepted in his own country. There were many widows in Israel, I can assure you, in Elijah's day when heaven remained shut for three years and six months, and a great famine raged throughout the land. But Elijah was not sent to any one of these; he was sent to a widow of Zarephath, a Sidonian town. In the prophet Elijah's time, there were many lepers in Israel, but none of these were cured except the Syrian Naaman" (Luke 4:24–27).

In those times, the prophet was primarily a wonder worker who did the marvelous signs of God. Because of this, the gospels make a comparison between the signs of Jesus and those of Elijah (Matthew 9:36–1 Kings 22:17; Mark 1:24–1 Kings 17:18). In the case of the son of the widow of Naim, for example, all recognized the analogy with the miracle of Elijah (1 Kings 17:23). Full of fear, all praised God with these words: "A great prophet has appeared among us," and "God has visited his people" (Luke 7:16).

On the other hand, the prophet was also the man who announced the coming of God; in this sense also, Jesus resembled the prophets. He announced the coming of the kingdom (Mark 1:15), and asked for conversion as a preparation for this coming. All that he did, he did as the prophets would have done. He went through the roads and the cities proclaiming this message: " 'Let us go elsewhere to the neighboring country towns so that I can preach there too, because that is why I came.' And he went all through Galilee preaching in their synagogues and casting out devils" (Mark 1:38–39).

As a preacher of penance, Jesus evoked the figure of the prophet Jonah: "On judgment day, the men of Nineveh will stand up with this generation and condemn it, because when Jonah preached, they repented; and there is something greater than Jonah here" (Matthew 12:41). Is it not at all strange that on the day of the transfiguration, the prophets Elijah and Moses appeared side by side with Jesus (Mark 9:4). As for Moses, John's gospel is full of parallels between Jesus and Moses.

In the persecutions too there was a similarity between Jesus and the prophets: "Jerusalem, Jerusalem, you that kill the prophets and stone those that are sent to you! How often have I longed to gather your children, as a hen gathers her chicks under her wings" (Matthew 23:37).

However, even though accepting the comparison to the prophets, Jesus knew himself to be superior to them: He was greater than Elijah, greater than Jonah. In the controversies with the scribes, he affirmed himself greater than Moses himself. Moses is the legislator of Israel and the founder of the law. In spite of this Jesus claimed authority sufficient to reinterpret and to complete the law of Moses. He did this work not as a commentator, but as one who had the right to complete it. "They went as far as Capernaum, and as soon as the Sabbath came he went to the synagogue and began to teach. And his teaching made a deep impression on them because, unlike the scribes, he taught them with authority" (Mark 1:21-22).

Consequently, in the question of the repudiation of a wife, the Pharisees invoked the authority of Moses, who permitted them to write an act of divorce. As we have said, Jesus replied that Moses had permitted it because "you were so unteachable that he wrote this commandment," and he added, "but from the beginning of creation God made them male and female. This is why a man must leave father and mother, and the two must become one body. So then, what God has united, man must not divide" (Mark 10:5-10).

In a similar way, Matthew united in the

Sermon on the Mount a series of questions and answers taken from the law of Moses: "You have heard that it was said to the ancients (that is, by Moses) . . . (Matthew 5:21, 24, 31, 33, 38, 43). "But, I say to you . . . be perfect as your Father is perfect." Jesus did not contradict the law. He commanded that it be perfected. "I tell you, unless your holiness surpasses that of the scribes and Pharisees you shall not enter the kingdom of God" (Matthew 5:20). Jesus completed what Moses said, and consequently he was at least as great as Moses.

In fact, Jesus had such authority over the Scriptures that he could sovereignly interpret all the books. Not only did he place himself on the level of Moses, the prophet and legislator, or on the level of the other prophets; he invoked with authority the writing of Solomon and proclaimed himself superior to Solomon: "On judgment day, the Queen of the South will rise with this generation and condemn it because she came from the ends of the earth to hear the wisdom of Solomon; and there is something greater than Solomon here" (Matthew 12:42). He clearly showed that he thought himself superior to David in the comment he made about Psalm 110:1: "If David addresses him as

'Lord,' in what sense can he be his son?" (Mark 12:37).

Still, no matter how it is understood, the title of "prophet" does not exhaust the meaning Jesus attributed to his mission. The people wanted to proclaim him king and to give him that title. They thought he must be the awaited one to whom was given the name of Messiah. Was he not the king?

## KING

Did Jesus ever pretend to be "king of the Jews," the Messiah awaited by the people? The gospels say that this was the crime invoked to condemn him. The inscription placed on the cross was so written: "The King of the Jews" (Mark 15:26). Near the cross, the priests and the scribes ridiculed him: "He saved others," they said, "he cannot save himself. Let the Christ, the 'King of Israel,' come down from the cross now, for us to see it and believe" (Mark 15:31–32). In the conviction of the priests and the scribes, Jesus was, naturally, a false Messiah.

Jesus was acclaimed by the people of Galilee

with this title of king. They did so at his entrance into Jerusalem. They received him triumphantly, even though they were simple people and the triumph was modest (Mark 2:1–2). Some Pharisees were scandalized, and they said to him: "Master, check your disciples" (Luke 19:39).

As a matter of fact, the disciples thought the very same thing of Jesus. He was the announced king, the king of whom the Scripture spoke, the Messiah of whom the people spoke. It was in this sense that Peter responded to Jesus: "You are the Christ" (that is, the Anointed, the King) (Mark 8:29). Because of this, Peter began to complain when Jesus introduced the theme of his death. This was also the reason the disciples wanted to know who would be the first in the kingdom of their king, and the sons of Zebedee asked for first place.

Many aspects of the mission of Jesus evoked the figure of the messianic king: the hope given to the poor, the health restored to the sick, and the expulsion of the demons. Why then did he not want this title proclaimed? Is it possible that he denied it? In truth, Jesus knew it was his lot to have an outstanding place in the kingdom of the Father. Nevertheless, he did not know either how or when. What he knew, and with ever-growing clarity and certainty, was the necessity of his death. Within his mission, there was no enthronement foreseen.

That is why he recommended silence on this point. After the declaration of Peter, Jesus "gave them strict orders not to tell anyone about him" (Mark 8:30). After the transfiguration, "As they came down the mountain he warned them to tell no one what they had seen until after the Son of Man had risen from the dead" (Mark 9:9). In the same manner, he prohibited the sick whom he cured and the demons whom he expelled to make a messianic proclamation.

The reason for this prohibition has provoked many commentaries. The problem, however, seems sufficiently clear, at least in the general lines. Jesus associated the prohibition with his foreknowledge of his death. He did not want to be acclaimed king, because he knew that to be crowned or anointed king of Israel was not his mission. He was a king in other ways. He knew his mission led toward persecution and death. He knew, of course, that there was a certain manner in which the title of king could be

applied to him, but not yet. It would come only
after he had fulfilled the essentials of his
mission.

## DEATH AND THE KINGDOM

In essence, Jesus knew his mission was very
brief and simple: to sow the seed and then to
die. In the kingdom of God, only the sowing of
the seed was asked of him. He would not see the
tree germinate and grow. He would know nothing of the tree before his death. Of the effects of
the word and the signs, of the results of so many
cures and of the efficacy of so many instructions, he would be allowed to gather absolutely
nothing. After he planted the seed, all that was
left for him to do was die. Death was the great
act the Father would ask of him, and only after
this ordeal would the seed he sowed take root
and flourish. This is why we have in the gospel
depiction of the life of Jesus the impression of a
race toward death. After a rapid entrance upon
his ministry and the enthusiasm of some
months over the signs he gave, the seed was
sown. Thereafter, all of Jesus' preoccupation
was directed to his unavoidable death. He

lived intensely this precarious phase of prophet, legislator, and wise man. He knew he would not have a long career.

Barely had he awakened hope when he disappeared. "Unless a wheat-grain falls on the ground and dies, it remains only a single grain. But if it dies, it yields a rich harvest" (John 12:24). It was not by chance Jesus chose the seed as a favorite theme for his parables.

Jesus lived in the anticipation of his death. How did he discover that this was his mission? Probably starting from Scripture. There is no gospel text in which he attributes to himself explicitly the title of "Servant of God," which corresponds to the figure of the man sacrificed for the good of the people in the prophecies of Isaiah 53. It seems, however, probable that he had really applied this prophecy to himself. The words pronounced in giving the chalice to the apostles at the Last Supper invoked clearly the prophecy of Isaiah's "Servant," "the blood of the covenant, to be poured out on behalf of many" (Mark 14:24–25).

In any event, when Jesus announced his death to his friends, he did so with much insistence. The fact that the gospels cite this announcement three times shows its importance.

Jesus, however, did not announce his death as an accident or a disgrace, as a fatality or as an inevitable consequence of his actions. If he had chosen to he could have avoided the conflict with the authorities. At least, he could have postponed the hour of conflict. He could have refrained from going to Jerusalem in the hour of greatest danger. It would have been easy to find refuge in a neighboring region, or simply in Galilee until the storm calmed. But everything happened as if, once he was conscious of the inevitability of death, Jesus had resolved to hasten the final outcome. He went to Jerusalem literally to give himself up. The disciples knew it (John 12:7–8) and attempted to divert him from going. But it was useless. So in their name, Thomas with much presumption said, "Let us go along, and die with him" (John 11:16).

Jesus foresaw his death as part, in fact, as the *principal* part, of his mission. Once the seed was planted, why wait any longer? As he said to Judas: "What you are going to do, do quickly" (John 13:27).

Surely this death has significance in the plan of the New Covenant. Much later the primitive Christian community would elaborate on its significance. But for the time being, Jesus lived the expectation of it with little theological elaboration. It was not necessary to compose a theological justification to give meaning to his death. He saw it simply as the acceptance of a mysterious plan related to the history of humanity.

"He began to teach them that the Son of Man was destined to suffer grievously, to be rejected by the elders, and the chief priests, and the scribes, and to be put to death, and after three days to rise again" (Mark 8:31). This formulation is very schematic and was obviously difficult for its gospel editor to accept. It reflected, however, the perception Jesus had of his death as an essential part of his mission. Mark repeats this prediction a second time. And then a third time, when Jesus went up to Jerusalem, he wrote: The disciples "were on the road, going up to Jerusalem; Jesus was walking on ahead of them; they were in a daze, and those who followed were apprehensive. Once more, taking the Twelve aside, he began to tell them what was going to happen to him. 'Now we are going up to Jerusalem, and the Son of Man is about to be handed over to the chief priests and the scribes. They will condemn him to death and will hand him over to the pagans, will mock him, and spit at him and scourge him, and put him to death, and after three days, he will rise again" (Mark 10:32–34). Again, of course, we perceive the hand of an author who narrates events after they had happened. However, the theme of the continual preoccupation of Jesus with his coming death is still there.

For Jesus, death would be a baptism, a purification, a passage to a new life, a total change: "Can you drink the cup that I must drink, or be baptized with the baptism with which I must be baptized?" (Mark 10:38).

The narrations of the death of Jesus constitute a very distinct part of the gospels. They are composed of solemn texts with all the appearances of a liturgical drama. Everything leads one to believe that the narrations themselves were formed in the context of the primitive Christian liturgy. The apostles themselves confess that they had fled. Therefore there were no worthwhile trusty observers at the events. The theological flavor is particularly strong. Everything underlines just one idea: Jesus entered into death as though into a mystery. In spite of being deprived of any mystical experience, he lived this mystery as his fundamental work, as one who saw it as the work of his life. He passed the night searching. He did not see any light, but he went on to the end. In the end, he said: "It is accomplished" (John 19:30). These words which John attributed to him show the full sense of his attitude. His was a drama he must follow to the end. The Father would do the rest. Even at the point of death, he entrusted the unifying of his work to the Father. He could not know in any way what was to come of all this. But he knew the Father knew.

In dying, Jesus sank to the very depths of loneliness. The rejection by the authorities, the silence of the people, the flight of the disciples, the denial of Peter, and the betrayal of Judas: the gospels accentuate the degree of this fall into abandonment. Finally, God himself seemed to withdraw his presence: "My God, my God, why have you deserted me?" (Mark 15:34) are the words the liturgical drama places on the lips of Jesus on the cross.

In dying, Jesus ascended to the very pinnacle of liberty. The gospels call attention to the fact that he went voluntarily to the encounter with death. Knowing that it was written in the Scriptures, he did not want a way out. He accepted his mission even to the end, as the hymn quoted in the epistle to the Philippians sings: "His state was divine, yet he did not cling to his equality with God, but emptied himself to assume the condition of a slave, and became as men are; and being as all men are, he was humbler yet, even to accepting death, death on a cross!" (Philippians 2:6–8).

In death, Jesus was the manifestation of God's love. John says: "God's love for us was revealed when he sent into the world his only Son, so that we could have life through him; this is the love I mean: not our love for God, but God's love for us when he sent his Son to be the sacrifice that takes our sins away" (1 John 4:9–10).

## JUDGE

How did Jesus understand the things that were to happen after his death? To answer this, we must cling only to the experience of those who were on hand prior to the resurrection, and do so in the context of the oldest documents. Here there is nothing that permits us to think that Jesus imagined his resurrection in the way he in fact experienced it. The most ancient texts are very careful about this.

In the first place, Jesus did not think his role

would be terminated with death. Even before the event, he announced to the disciples his participation in the final judgment. He placed himself in the center of the eschatological and apocalyptic perspective of the final judgment and of the final separation of people. Therefore, he must rise himself one day to judge all. We already said he probably thought the day of this judgment was not very distant. Consequently, having thought of his resurrection in terms of participation in the judgment, this resurrection would come soon. The time of absence would be brief.

In speaking of his role in the final judgment, Jesus used the title, "Son of Man." He never once said "I." Always he said "the Son of Man," even if the context clearly showed he was speaking of himself. As a matter of fact, even to announce his death, Jesus used the same indirect way of speaking of himself.

The title "Son of Man" was not common in Judaism. It was encountered in certain texts of the Old Testament and in some Apocrypha. The most celebrated texts were Daniel 7 and 10, and the Apocrypal book of Enoch. In both texts, "Son of Man" designated a glorious one

who would appear at the end of time in a context of victory and judgment. In different
places of the New Testament, it seems to have a
certain reference to Chapter 7 of Daniel.

In the synoptic gospels, the title "Son of
Man" appears seventy times. It is always used
by Jesus (or almost always, since there are some
disputed texts) and always he is obviously
speaking of himself. Jesus did not apply any
other title to himself alone. Others did not so
address him. In this fact, there is a very curious
linguistic originality.

Its use was so extraordinary that it would be
difficult to think of it as theological elaboration of the text by the primitive Christian
community. The gospels use the title because
the title is a memory of how Jesus spoke of
himself. In the churches where Greek was
spoken, the title must have been incomprehensible, and must have stood out in a quite exqui-
site way, exactly as it does today. In the church
it has disappeared from everyday use.

Jesus gave himself this title first as much to
emphasize his weakness as his greatness. On
one hand he said: "The Son of Man has nowhere to lay his head" (Matthew 8:20), and

"the Son of Man came not to be served, but to serve" (Matthew 8:28). On the other hand, he said: "The Son of Man has authority on earth to forgive sins" (Mark 2:10), and "the Son of Man is master even of the sabbath" (Mark 2:28).

Later, the phrase "Son of Man" is invoked to announce the death of Jesus: "He began to teach them that the Son of Man had to suffer grievously," etc. (Mark 8:31); "the Son of Man will be delivered into the hands of men" (Mark 9:31); "the Son of Man is about to be handed over to the chief priests and the scribes" (Mark 10:33).

This same title also served to announce the future manifestations of Jesus in the role of Judge. It is clear that this way of speaking indicated that Jesus saw the function of future judge as part of his mission and the continuation of his ministry exercised in death. The announcements of the coming of the judge are well known.

If anyone in this adulterous and sinful generation is ashamed of me and of my words, the Son of Man will also be ashamed of him when he comes in the glory of his Father with the holy angels (Mark 8:38).

I tell you solemnly, when all is made new and the Son of Man sits on his throne of glory, you will yourselves sit on twelve thrones, to judge the twelve tribes of Israel (Matthew 19:28).

The Son of Man will send his angels and they will gather, out of his kingdom, all things that provoke offenses, and all who do evil (Matthew 13:41).

And then they will see the Son of Man coming in the clouds, with great power and glory; then, too, he will send the angels to gather his chosen from the four winds, from the ends of the world to the ends of heaven (Mark 13:26–27).

Finally, the famous declaration that the synoptic tradition put on the lips of Jesus in the midst of the tribunal of the Jews: "The high priest put a second question to him, 'Are you the Christ,' he said, 'the Son of the Blessed One?' 'I am,' said Jesus, 'and you will see the Son of Man seated at the right hand of the Power and coming with the clouds of heaven' " (Mark 14:61–62).

The personality of the Son of Man remains a mystery. The attributes which are given to him in this quotation are only citations of Daniel, and therefore they served to hide more than reveal the qualities of the "Son of Man."

In any event, Jesus foresaw the end of history. Of all his work apparently nothing would remain. Still, he knew that the Father reserved a final victory for him. The words pronounced by Jesus, the acts manifested by him would not be in vain; at least they would be revealed at the end of time in a judgment of humanity—as the criteria to separate the cockle from the wheat, the good fish from the bad.

## THE TIME OF THE CHURCH

In regard to the time that separated the death of Jesus from the manifestation of the future judge, we can ask ourselves if Jesus himself had any idea of the role he was to have in it. We have already said that he did not think this interval would be very long. Therefore, the question of that role, which for us is fundamental, had no importance for him. We know very well the effort that the primitive church made to understand and to reconcile the teachings of Jesus within the perspective of "delay" of the approaching end. It was the fundamental problem of the first Christian century. In a certain manner, it is perhaps still the first—perhaps the only—truly theological problem.

Had Jesus foreseen an anticipated resurrection three days after death, as was said by the apostles? We do not know. Perhaps he did, in a confused way. In any event, no clear indication appears. The three prophecies of the passion and the resurrection were later additions, as all independent interpreters agree.

It seems certain that Jesus foresaw his presence in the midst of the disciples during the time of the mission: "Where two or three are gathered in my name, there am I in their midst" (Matthew 18:20). The mode of this presence was not determined. Nevertheless, we cannot attribute to the consciousness of Jesus before the passion that which John attributes to him, and which constitutes a theological development that began with the spiritual illumination after the resurrection. Nor can we believe that Jesus knew before dying what the gospels attribute to him as words pronounced after the resurrection.

In what he said about the church, it is clear Jesus did not foresee the church as it is today. He could not even conceive of what the church was to become at the end of the first century. All he said about the mission to the nations, he entrusted to the disciples. Consequently, the organization of the church was entirely their burden, and, in a special way, that of the twelve and Peter. This is why the structures of the Church can be so flexible. Beyond the institution of the Supper—as a supper, not as a liturgy—almost nothing was commanded by Jesus. Consequently, almost everything in the church is open to evolution, if the church finds evolution useful to fulfill the mission that is incumbent on it. Never was there a founder so liberal to his successors as Jesus was. He entrusted to them all the organizing. He only left one very clear principle: that the organization would always be subordinate to love and to humility. What Jesus left to the disciples as a recommendation gives the final stamp to his work. Of these recommendations, the gospels made small collections which are presented as parallels (Mark 9:33–50; Matthew 18:1–35; Luke 9:43–50): "If anyone wants to be first, he must make himself last of all and servant of all" (Mark 9:35). "Anyone who is not against us is for us" (Mark 9:40). "If your hand should cause you to sin, cut it off!" (Mark 9:43). "Salt is a good thing, but if salt has become insipid, how can you season it again? Have salt in yourselves, and be at peace with one another" (Mark 9:50).

The discourses in John particularly, after the Last Supper, developed these themes. In washing the feet of the disciples on his last night, Jesus explained to them the significance of the gesture for the future Church: "If I, the Lord and Master, have washed your feet, you should wash each other's feet. I have given you an example, so that you may copy what I have done to you. I solemnly tell you, no servant is greater than the master, no messenger is greater than the man who sent him" (John 13:14–16).

With this we will conclude these meditations: "No servant is greater than his master. . . . Now that you know all this, happiness will be yours, if you behave accordingly" (John 13:16–17).